The Divinity Factor

by Donald L. Hicks

MOUNTAIN
PUBLISHING

PO Box 754
Huntsville, AR 72740
www.ozarkmt.com

For permission, or serialization, condensation, adaptions, or for catalog of other publications, write to: Ozark Mountain Publishing, Inc., P.O. Box 754, Huntsville, AR 72740, Attn: Permissions Department.

Quote from CONVERSATIONS WITH GOD by Neale Donald Walsch, Copyright © 1995 by Neale Donald Walsch. Used by permission of G. P. Putnam's Sons, a division of Penguin Group (USA) Inc.

Quote from LIFE AFTER LIFE by Raymond A Moody, Jr., M.D., Copyright © 1975 by Raymond A. Moody, Jr., M.D., **used by permission of Raymond A. Moody, Jr., M.D.**

Library of Congress Cataloging-in-Publication Data
Hicks, Donald L. - 1962-
"The Divinity Factor" by Donald L. Hicks
Step by step instructions on how to use the 6 laws of the universe to create anything you want in your life.
1. Metaphysics   2. Manifestation   3. Philosophy
I. Hicks, Donald L., 1962   II. Title   III. Metaphysics

Library of Congress Catalog Card Number: 2005935758
ISBN: 1-886940-91-6

Cover Art and Layout by www.enki3d.com
Book Design: Julia Degan
Book Set in: Baskerville Old Face, Times New Roman

Published By

OZARK
MOUNTAIN
PUBLISHING

PO Box 754
Huntsville, AR 72740
www.ozarkmt.com
Printed in the United States of America

TABLE OF CONTENTS

A Note from the Author

In the 1980's, during an era my wife and I call our "child-rearing" years, she and I had a special dream. Because we both were avid readers, because we each enjoyed dabbling with writing, and because we both enjoyed rubbing elbows and chatting with other "book people", our dream was to someday own a bookstore. Coming from poor mid-west families, neither of us had grandiose aspirations of opening a bookstore and then cloning out nationwide locations to compete with Barnes and Noble or Borders. Instead, our goal was simple. We merely wanted to open a "Ma and Pa" store that could afford us a quiet life, while keeping at least one slice of lightly-molded bread on the table.

With three children at home, however, having hungry mouths to feed, clothing to buy, non-ending piles of laundry to hose off, dishes that appeared to be "self-dirtying", and bills that multiplied faster than rabbits on Viagra, our dream seemed to be outdistancing reality.

By the 1990's, as our children neared the age of maturity, our dream appeared no closer. While the self-dirtying dishes and laundry-compost piles remained (unabating), the maintenance costs of bicycles was replaced by that of cars. The bills had festered into life forms of their own, and the phones seemed to ring incessantly.

We knew life was getting better, however, because the science projects now resulted in much fewer fires, with only the occasional explosion.

It was at about this point in life – the critical mass – that we discovered *The Divinity Factor.*

In late 1995, after our last child had flown the coop, my wife and I were finally able to realize our dream by opening a modest

i

bookstore. We began this venture by building several bookshelves and purchasing the inventory of an out-of-town bookseller who was closing. We then leased a retail space, and began eagerly drafting blueprints.

In designing the store, our goal was to create an ambiance of coziness, while still allowing foot-traffic to flow. We wanted to place related genres together, so if a shopper came in looking for diet books, they might also see "low-fat cook books" in the "Cookbook" section, while also seeing "weight-loss/exercise books" in the "Fitness" Section.

To accomplish our objective, we first divided the store into a "fiction area" and a "non-fiction area", then went about arranging the genres in either section.

The dilemma arose when we reached the genres of "Spirituality", "Occult", and "Religion". By default, these genres fall into a "grey-area" for booksellers. They are neither the fact-based recounts of "non-fiction", nor are they the colorful tales of "fiction". Books such as these are based on the beliefs and personal experiences of one or more individuals: beliefs and experiences that may be sustained by multitudes, yet often cannot be proven nor disproven by science.

The reason I mention this as a prelude to *The Divinity Factor* is to make an important point. As the author, I view *The Divinity Factor* as a blend of religion and non-fiction. It is like a plant that's potted in belief, yet is rooted in the soil of science. It is an alchemy of spiritual transcendence, a candle in darkness, chasing away Life's shadows and questions.

As you will see, together we can make the world a brighter and better place. This process begins with each individual, yet works on a collective basis, like the lilies of the field that sprout and choke away weeds.

Before we launch our journey, I'd like to share a few of my own beliefs and set the stage. These beliefs have come to me through a life-long communion with God, and through tangible experiences in my own life:

.

- There is one "God" – whom I prefer to call "God", but answers to many names. He is known by: Allah, Almighty, Buddha, Creator, Diana, Elohim, God, Jehovah, Yahweh, and many others. Most fittingly, He may be known simply as "I Am": the state of everlasting existence.
- God – the One God – created everything from Himself. He is the purest and most quintessential form of energy, and is *everything* at a sub-atomic level (including you and I).
- Since energy is eternal, and we are made by God (who is also energy), we are *all* eternal by default.
- Within each of us, there is power through the divine energy of God. This energy level governs our outlook of life (our emotions), and our craving for this energy unwittingly drives our desires. As our energy is shared or stolen among us, our individual reserves can fluctuate. Unknowingly, we mistake "power, money, and sex" as the primary motivations within life, not realizing we crave these things because they enable us to acquire divine energy.
- God wants us to be happy and enjoy our experience of life. He constantly guides us. We need only "listen" to Him through one of the many methods He uses to communicate with us (as will be explained).
- Being Divine by nature, we have the innate ability to manifest our own destiny and live as abundantly as we each desire. In plain terms, we can create *anything* we wish to own and experience. "Matter" is malleable to our will. We also have the ability to heal and perform "miracles" through our

connection with God. This is a lesson we have been told many, many times, but have not comprehended. We continually ignore it as "too good to be true".

- There is no "right" or "wrong" in Life; only actions and consequences. God does not "judge" nor set one standard for Himself, and another for us. He has merely given us rules for our own safety – rules to protect us from ourselves until we understand our own abilities and powers.
- *Love* is the greatest gift we can give.
- *Fear* is the negative emotion that brings *every traceable hardship into our life.* Only love can free us from fear. Fear causes us to cower in the shadows; Love allows us to dance in the sunlight.
- Since all life forms (literally) share the energy of God, all life is sacred and should be loved and appreciated.
- Whenever we show appreciation and respect to any living thing, we in fact "praise God", and that appreciation comes back to us three-fold.

In the upcoming pages, the foundations for these beliefs will be laid forth so you can "test" and witness them in your own life.

I invite you to journey on.

Preface

Within each of us lies a Divine power. We can be blissfully happy, live in abundance, love and be loved, and have everything we ever need.

To tap this power, there is nothing to buy or save for; nothing to fear you might lose. You already have the latent ability to *live your dreams today.* This power is your quintessential essence and your own Divinity. It is, and will always be, within you. It can never be taken away.

As you will see in the upcoming pages, by learning to commune with God and tap your shared Divinity, you can find happiness, fulfill dreams, and have *anything* you desire.

Anything at all.

If you want a new house, you can have it. If you want better health, you can have it. Whether it's money, deeper relationships, better sex, or general happiness, it is all within your grasp. All you need to do is follow the steps provided in this book; steps that Man has been shown countless times, but did not correctly interpret. Steps that are simply and thoroughly explained in the upcoming pages.

Through this book, you will learn the hidden motivations that drive personal relationships and cause us to do the sometimes crazy things we do. You will emerge from this spiritual baptism with a fuller, deeper understanding of the world around you, *knowing* exactly how to request what you want, and how to avoid what you don't.

God has given us all the tools we need to be happy. Moreover, He *wants* us to be happy. He has told us "we deserve it" and urges us to use the tools He has provided.

It is well within our grasp.

*For verily I say unto you, that whosoever shall say unto this mountain "be thou removed, and be thou cast into the sea"; and shall not doubt in his heart, but shall believe that those things which he saith shall come to pass; **he shall have whatever he saith.***
*Therefore I say unto you, **what things soever ye desire**, when ye pray, **believe that ye receive them, and ye shall receive them.***

Mark 11: 23, 24
The Bible,
KJV

Part One

Chapter 1
The Farm Parable

To launch our adventure, I've written a brief parable that's printed below. As we pass through the upcoming pages, I will occasionally use "parables" to make certain points.

The reason I've chosen to incorporate parables is very simple: when correctly written, parables are multi-dimensional. That is, if you're in one frame of mind, you may read a parable and get *one specific message*. However, if you're in another frame of mind, you can read the *same* parable, yet learn something completely different. As we progress, this will be demonstrated. We'll refer back to these parables to show "other sides of the coin". These parables will each be named, and an interpretation will always follow, making it easy to grasp their meaning and relevance.

The Farm Parable:

On a sunny July day, a young boy followed his father into their farm's chicken house.

The boy, Johnny, had just turned six. He had recently learned to count to 100; a feat that made him quite proud.

Entering the chicken house, the father walked past a row of ten chicken boxes, briefly shooing a hen from each box and scanning the nests. He then pulled a pen from his pocket and wrote a number in the palm of his hand.

"Tell me how many eggs there are, Johnny," the father said.

Starting at the first box, Johnny began counting the eggs. After he reached the 5th box, he lost count and had to start over. Trying again, he started at the first box and concentrated, being careful not to lose count this time. A moment later, after working his way down the row of boxes, he turned and proudly announced his finding: "50".

Upon that note, the father turned his palm to Johnny, revealing the number "50".

Face aglow with wonderment, Johnny asked: "Wow! How did you count so fast? I didn't even see you counting..."

"I didn't count," the father replied. "There were 5 eggs in each of the 10 nests. I simply multiplied."

Through this first parable, we obtain a simple lesson. When learning any worthwhile process, we must first learn the basics before we tackle the final product.

Math is a suitable example.

When we begin to study math, we are first taught what numbers represent. After we have a basic understanding of this representation – of how numbers represent quantities – we can then learn to count. After we've learned to count, we then learn to add (thus reducing the counting process to a simpler form). We then learn "reverse counting" (subtraction). Then multiplication. Then division. Algebra. And so on.

While children as young as Johnny can be taught to memorize the multiplication tables, it serves in the child's best interest to learn *in a progressive order.* By doing so, when they reach the more complex tasks (such as multiplication), they can comprehend the value and underlying mechanics of the process.

Our lesson here runs along the same lines. As your guide on this journey, I could easily teach you the "multiplication tables" for getting what you want from the universe to be happy. You could read the steps, and in most cases accomplish the desired result. The underlying problem, however, would be one of *comprehension* and *faith.* You would never know *why* the Divinity system worked, nor understand the mechanics. And at certain times, it would fail inexplicably.

Yet most importantly, you might also request the *wrong* things by defying Universal Laws, which would inevitably bring you more discontentment than joy.

So before we learn to "multiply" and start receiving what God is offering, let's take a little time to learn the basics. A happy future awaits nearby.

Life's Puzzle

Life is the grandest picture puzzle of all.

Whenever you launch any new journey, it's critical to know W*here You Are Now* before you can plot a course to W*here You Want To Be*. It also helps to know W*here You Have Been* to understand how you arrived at W*here You Are Now*. Knowing W*here You Have Been* may also cast insight into *why* you have chosen a desired destination.

As an example, if you're traveling through Florida because you want to visit Orlando, having a Florida road map won't help unless you know W*here You Are Now*. If you think you're in Miami, when you're really in Tallahassee, there's a good chance you'll venture out in the *wrong direction*. If you pass a "Welcome to Tallahassee" sign as you reach for your map, however, you'll know *your present location* because of *the past*. Moreover, if you also recall spending the last ten years in bitter Alaska, dreaming of visiting Florida's theme parks from your igloo, it may lend insight into *why* you chose Orlando as your present destination.

While our journey here focuses on "finding our own Divinity" (instead of a map point), the same principal holds true. Before we can plot a course toward Divine Living, we must first establish W*here We Are Now*. In doing so, we need to know W*here We Have Been*.

In establishing W*here We Have Been*, I could tell you now that we are all parts of God, that we have *always* existed, and we

4

always *will* exist, but using such a broad and expansive road map would be of little service. This would be like trying to use a world globe to navigate from Tallahassee to Orlando. Instead of using such a broad base, we need to focus down to our present "country" and "state", starting with *this* lifetime, incorporating your own involvement.

To begin, we can establish a common thread that all readers share. At some nonspecific point during each life, we are each presented with certain questions. These questions commonly are:

"What is my purpose in life?"
"Why am I here?"
"And what is life all about?"

As you'll see later, there is an underlying reason we each are given these questions. That reason, now, however, need not impede us. What is more critical at this moment is understanding the impact these questions have on us when they are discovered.

When we are presented with "Life's Questions", it's the equivalent of the child finding a picture puzzle that has been dumped into a pile. As the child begins to seek answers and pick through the various pieces of Life's puzzle, he or she sees graphics on each piece. The child senses a larger and meaningful picture will be revealed when the pieces are assembled. Yet while studying each piece separately, the child can only imagine and wonder what that picture might be.

As the child begins to assemble the puzzle, he or she soon becomes overwhelmed by the complexity of the task. The newness of Life is seductively enticing and the child is coaxed away – at least until some plaguing Life issue causes us – the child – to return to the puzzle.

I think I'm safe in saying that most people can relate to this phenomenon. We seldom question the purpose of life when our world is sunny and bright. This question tends to hide itself during pleasant sailing, only rearing its face during the deepest and darkest travails, when the gales of stormy weather have fallen. When a loved one passes, when we lose a job, when bill collectors are calling non-stop, or when some other hurricane of distress creeps over the horizon, we find ourselves questioning the purpose of living.

I'm going to tell you a secret now that won't make much sense, but will fall into place much later in this journey:

We bring these "storms of life" upon ourselves to remind us of this question, forcing ourselves to return to the puzzle.

With each Life Issue that arises, we piece together a little more of the puzzle; often constructing the border, or building little "islands of pieces" that do not yet connect with the frame of the puzzle. Through this "on/off" process, we assemble more and more of the puzzle and continually gain insights into the overall picture.

This brings us to W*here You Are Now.*

You are a spiritual being who has lived many lifetimes, and has completed many puzzles. In the past, you've solved those puzzles and were able to advance to a higher level of learning. Now, however, you have a new, much more difficult puzzle at hand.

The good news is, God understands this and wants to help.

It is no coincidence you are reading this book. Whether it was suggested to you by a friend, the cover peaked your curiosity, you are feeling an *unexplainable sense of restlessness*, or you merely want to feel closer to God, there is a specific *reason* or *purpose* this book landed in your hands. God – not myself, nor the publisher, nor the bookseller – has directed you here so that He might aid you in assembling your Life Puzzle.

God loves you and wants you to be happy. You have sought, and in His magnificence: *He is answering.*

As we work together on this project, I ask you to be aware there *may* be times when gaps and unconnected puzzle-piece "islands" appear to exist. There may also be moments when the topics seem very "disjointed", out of place, or muddy before becoming clear. In a way, attempting to describe the "whole picture" of Life is akin to defining how colors are formed. In certain instances, one cannot define a given color until another color has been mentioned. As an example, one can't explain "green" until after they have defined the "blue" and "yellow" bases that create green. Yet while describing the various shades of blue and yellow (such as teal or lemon-lime), one may need to reference "green" – before it has been defined.

Such is the case with Life's puzzle.

Since we are each different, and may have focused on different parts of our own puzzle – different "colors" of life – the assembly of each puzzle is unique for each person. When the last pieces fall into place, however, you will know it. You will emerge with a complete understanding that God loves us, He is ALWAYS with us, He wants us to be happy, and He has given us all the tools we need to accomplish that end.

We can have anything we want. Our mission in life is to experience – and do so with love, and only love.

Chapter 2
Understanding Energy

Okay. We've reached the point where, before we can move forward, we need to *unlearn* one of the things we think we "know".

In the early 1900's, Albert Einstein made a startling discovery. In the act of trying to identify the most elementary building block of matter, working on the heels of Max Planck's Quanta Theory[1], Einstein discovered that *all matter is comprised of energy at a sub-atomic level.*

For those of us who aren't pursuing a career in quantum physics, let's look at this in layman's terms with very loose definitions. Suppose you had an electronic microscope in front of you, and you slip a small piece of paper onto the microscope's slide. As you look into the eyepiece, you can see the porous surface of the paper and any microscopic mites and bacteria living there (some resemble alien creatures, so beware before you look). Turning up the magnification and peering deeper, you begin to see the wood cells clinging together. And as you look even deeper, passing molecules and looking *into* atoms, you begin to see sub-atomic particles. These atoms lend the impression of small solar systems (and may be the origin of those alien creatures you saw on the paper's surface).

A problem arises, however, when you try to look *into* these sub-atomic particles. As you continue to power-up the microscope, the particles become "wavy" and are no longer solid. They appear like heat-waves or water-filled petri dishes. Moreover, these particles stop behaving like "matter" altogether and take on the characteristics of waves and energy. They hold positive, negative, and neutral charges, and are indeed, energy.[2] *They can even be influenced by our thoughts.*

What Einstein and several early twentieth-century scientists helped to prove, is that the book you are now holding is formed by billions and billions of tiny energy particles which have clumped together. In effect, this book is made of energy. If you are sitting in a chair, that chair is also made up of energy. The floor beneath your chair is also made of energy. The ground beneath you is energy. Your body is energy, and your thoughts are energy. Everything we see, hear, taste, smell, or feel is a form of energy.

If you're a "Trekkie", you might compare life to living on the "holo-deck". All things, whether they are tangible or intangible – whether it's sunlight, or wind, or solid granite – are energy at a sub-atomic level. All "things" are merely energy in different states.

Energy is the most elementary building block of *all* things.

To look at this phenomena in a life-size example – one we can all relate to and see without a microscope – we need only look at water. At room temperature, water is a liquid. When boiled, it becomes steam. When subjected to temperatures below 32 degrees Fahrenheit, it freezes and becomes "solid matter"; so solid we can walk on it and need a pick to break it apart.

10

All matter works on this same principle. If a lump of coal is cast into a fire, it becomes nothing more than dissipated heat and ashes that can be scattered by the wind. Yet if the same coal is subjected to sufficient pressure, it becomes a diamond.

Most simply put, all matter is *energy at rest.*

I don't want the following part to disturb you, but I do want to make you *think* to promote the "relearning" process. In our busy world, with honking horns, demanding schedules, and people bustling this way and that, it's all too easy to overlook what energy and nature are doing all around us. We are in the middle of an energy *maelstrom*; a world far more bustling than we are aware, and most of the time we are completely oblivious to this "underworld". Wherever you are at this very moment, there are radio-waves bouncing all around you. If you have a radio nearby, you can easily prove this to yourself by turning on the radio and tuning in a local station. There are signals in the air for hundreds of AM stations; and hundreds more for FM stations. There are television signals, the transmissions of CB radios, Ham radios, satellite signals, infrared, microwaves, and the neighbor next door may be talking *through* you on their cell phone. X-rays can pass through you. Light and shadows play all around us at every moment. The air moves, exchanging heat and cold, yet we seldom notice the stirring unless we feel a cold draft or smell a wafting odor.

At first, the concept of *all things* being made of energy is very difficult to grasp. It's like trying to comprehend infinity, with time stretching so far into the future it eventually fades from sight. Our difficulty with this concept comes from erroneously perceiving "matter" as "solid mass" formed from "solid" particles, while perceiving "energy" as being primarily invisible, and usually intangible.

11

Gravity is a good example of our perception of energy. While we clearly feel the *effects* of gravity, we can't see it or taste it.

Light is another example. We may see sunlight or feel its warmth on our skin, but it's not a tactile substance.

Nor can we touch all those sound waves bouncing around the room. We can't even see them. But if we turn on a radio or TV set, we know this energy is present.

We can't see electricity either, but if we stick a bobby pin into a live electric socket, we'll definitely know it's there (although I would advise against such action unless you have a penchant for near death experiences...or the real thing).

It will take some time for you to grasp the concept of *all things being formed of energy*. This is one of those "island" puzzle pieces I mentioned earlier. We've snapped several pieces of our puzzle together, laid this little "puzzle-piece island" in the middle of our frame, but it doesn't yet connect to the border.

It will, however, as your lessons here progress.

As you begin to see how the parts of the universe work together – how these energies subtly flow and interact – how matter becomes energy and energy becomes matter – and how people subconsciously work with this energy, never realizing it – you will see the truth and feel it in your heart.

Modern science itself, is currently exploring this same "puzzle-piece island". In the December, 1997 issue of Discover Magazine, in an article written by Jeffrey Winters (*"Let There Be Matter"*, pg. 40) we find the following:

"But like any equation, E=mc² works in both directions.... That is, it should be possible to convert energy into matter. Now a team of physicists has accomplished just that: they have transmuted light into matter.
"We're able to turn optical photons into matter," says Princeton physicist Kirk McDonald, co-leader of the team. "That is quite a technological leap."

What you will soon learn is, we can each already do this using Divine energy and the power of our thoughts. We already have the ability – through God – to turn "energy" into "matter".

As you're grappling with this, here's a thought to ponder:

In the time *before* creation, before the planets and space were formed, before there was *anything* except God in existence – if you *were* God, and you were *everything* at that time, what "material" would you use to make the planets, the beasts of the earth, light, winds, man, and all other elements?

If you were *everything*, would that material not be yourself?

Hereby know that we dwell in Him, and He in us, because He hath given us of His Spirit.
1 John 4:12
The Bible
KJV

*So God created man in his **own** image, in the **image of God** created he him; male and female he created them.*
Genesis 1:27
The Bible
KJV

13

Science tells us that all things are made from Energy. Religion tells us all things come from God. Moreover, it tells us God is with us, in us, and in our midst at all times. God *is* all things, and all things *are* God. This is the first lesson we must learn.

The First Law of the Universe is this:

All things are made of Energy. This energy *is* God.

Chapter 3
The Energy in People

Okay. Ready for another parable to advance us along?

As with *The Farm Parable*, we'll be referring back to the following parable much later, so please keep it in mind.

<u>*The Parable of the Lovers*</u>:

In the middle of a shopping trip, while taking a break between stores, Jane sat down on a bench in the main corridor of the local shopping mall.

Being an author, people-watching was one of Jane's favorite pastimes. Seeing people often sparked an idea for a new character in her young-adult romance novels. In some cases, just by watching people, she could conceive a whole story. Her last novel "Different Desires" had resulted from just such an incidence. She had conceived the whole plot while sitting on the same mall bench. It came to her in a flash, when she had observed a computer geek (replete with the horn-rimmed glasses) who accidentally bumped into a pink-haired gothic girl (replete with the black lipstick, green nail polish, and torn black fish-net stockings). In real life, the two had done little more than exchange irritated looks; but in "Different Desires", there had been "instant magic".

15

Today, two different young lovers caught Jane's eye. They were walking through the mall, laughing, smiling, and pointing out window displays while holding hands – and one look told Jane that the couple was in love.

Thinking about it, Jane wondered how she knew with such certainty that the young couple was indeed, in love. After all, she didn't know either the young man or the young lady. She hadn't asked them if they were in love. She had never seen them before or spoken to them. As far as she knew, they could be a re-united brother and sister. Yet despite logic and reason, she knew–- with absolute certainty – that the couple were lovers.

Why?

How did she know?

How could she?

Intrigued, Jane continued to watch, knowing this phenomenon was something she needed to capture and put into words.

Aside from holding hands, the couple weren't touching. Nor were they walking overly close. It was something about their faces. A certain "glow", and a brightness in their eyes when they looked at each other. It was nearly tangible, yet this "glow" was subtly visible.

It dawned upon Jane that she had seen that same "glow" a week earlier, on her sister's face, the day of her sister's wedding.

The question was, what caused the "glow"?

Was it "love". And if so, was there a medical reason behind it?

16

Determined to find out, Jane left the mall. After returning home, she called her friend, Bill, who happened to be a doctor.

"I know the glow you're describing," Bill said. "I've seen it myself. And there's a medical explanation. It's the body's method of preparing for copulation. While readying for sex, the body goes through a host of actions. The heartbeat increases, hormones begin to flow, respiration increases, and a slight sweat can form on the skin, causing the appearance of this "glow". It's quite normal."

For reasons she couldn't understand, Jane doubted Bill's explanation. It didn't strike home. The answer sounded too pat, like he was merely repeating something learned from textbooks or med-school.

"But Bill, it's not like they were necking. They were just walking through the mall, holding hands."

"That may be true. But they might have been thinking about sex," he offered. "Who knows?"

"I guess that could be true." Jane lied. "Thanks for your help."

After hanging up the phone, Jane continued to ponder. The whole "readying for copulation" idea just didn't fit. The more she thought about it, the more wrong it felt. After all, her sister certainly wasn't "readying for copulation" 12 hours before the honeymoon would begin... not with her mind consumed by the worry of some unforeseen disaster spoiling the wedding.

And on the flip side, if what Bill said was true, why didn't "joggers" have the same glow? Wouldn't they also have increased blood flow, increased respiration, and a slight sweat on the skin? Perhaps they wouldn't have the same hormones flowing, but would those hormones alone cause the glow?

Beyond that, Jane realized something else. She had seen the same glow on the face of pregnant women.

Something was there. Jane could sense it.

And Jane was right.

Within each of us there is a Divine energy. It is the force that drives us, and the fuel for all thought, emotion, and activity. It moderates our mood and outlooks, and from there it shapes the fabric of our lives.

This divine energy – which I have dubbed "life force" – is the veritable essence of God. It is that which He used to create us, and the part of Him that resides in every life.

Like the radio waves that bounce silently and invisibly around us, God's divine energy is at work in every corner of existence. It is ever-present in our world, yet it is rarely seen or noticed. It is anonymous, yet unmistakably His. It is intractable, yet gently yielding to a child's cry. It is the catalyst of Creation; the purest of love.

As you will see in the upcoming chapters, it is this life force which causes lovers, pregnant women, and those who are otherwise *honored* or *esteemed* to "glow".

We each maintain a personal "reservoir" of this life force, and our own abundancy (or scarcity) is reflected in each life.

Unknowingly, we compete for life force. We exchange it with others, sometimes choosing to freely share, while at other times feeling we must "guard our reserve" and hoard. We steal it, and

18

have it stolen from us. We will lie for it, fight for it, and covet it without realizing what we are doing, or why.

So why do we so crave this life force?

A surprising answer awaits you.

Chapter 4
Transference of Life Force

Paying Attention - Giving

As we go about our day-to-day life, there are many ways that life force energy is transferred and shared among us.

Whenever we *openly* "pay" attention to another being – without "putting up our guard" – we are sharing our life force. The more life force energy we have, the better we feel. The better we feel, the more apt we are to share.

What will surprise you to learn is – *the more we share, the more our own life force grows.*

A common houseplant can provide us tangible proof of the "sharing" phenomenon. As most of us know, botany researchers have proven that plants flourish when people talk to them or play soft music.

I would pose to you a new foundation for your thoughts: The plants do not flourish because the music has "magical qualities" (although it is a form of energy – and it can energize plants to grow, just as it can provide us a boost of energy) – nor do plants improve because they are in a harmonic, peaceful atmosphere.

The plants do better because we are *paying attention to them.*

By going through the motions of setting up high-tech sound equipment, or by simply stopping by their pot and checking on them, we are sending the unspoken message: "we care".

By caring, we are sharing our own life force with the plant.

If you have a houseplant and want to try an experiment that will prove this, try the following:

Pick the poorest-looking houseplant you own (or buy one that needs a good home) and move it to a spot where it will still get some sun. Most importantly, place the plant where you will *notice* it several times a day. If you have a window above the kitchen sink, that may be the perfect place because you'll see the plant while cleaning up from meals – plus, it's close to water. If you don't have a kitchen window, the coffee table near your TV is another good location, provided it receives some sunlight.

I would advise against using a corner table or stand. Put the plant someplace *visible* and in the open.

After you've appropriately placed your plant, take a picture of the plant so you'll be able to see exactly how it looked *before* the experiment.

At least twice a day, take time to study the plant. As you do so, caress the leaves and try sending your plant the simple mental message that "you care". Do this for two weeks, watering the plant no more than normal, then compare how the plant looks opposed to the "before" picture.

In *The Secret Life of Plants³*, an account of the lives of plants and their spiritual interaction with Mankind and Nature, the authors discuss some fascinating research performed by Marcel Vogel and an assistant. Vogel, a scientist, was studying the effects of projecting thoughts and messages to plants. During his experiments, Vogel enlisted the aid of a spiritually gifted friend, Vivian Wiley, to help with his research. Following Vogel's instructions, Wiley plucked two leaves from a plant in her garden. After picking these leaves, she sat one aside and ignored it. The other she laid on her bedside table and, each day, she *willed* it to continue to live. A month into the experiment, the leaf she had ignored had shriveled and turned brown, while the leaf she had willed to live was:

"radiantly vital and green, just as if it had been freshly plucked from the garden".

Hoping to replicate the experiment, Vogel tried it on his own. Authors Tompkins and Bird recount the experiment as follows:

"...Vogel picked three leaves from an elm tree outside his IBM laboratory; at home, he laid them on a plate of glass near his bed.

Each day, before breakfast, Vogel stared concentratedly at the two outer leaves on the glass plate for about one minute, exhorting them lovingly to continue to live; the center leaf he assiduously ignored. In a week, the center leaf had turned brown and shriveled. The outer leaves were still green and healthy looking."

Vogel further proved his research by attaching a galvanometer (basically a polygraph machine) to a philodendron and recording the plant's reactions as he focused his energy toward the plant:

"Vogel stood before the plant, completely relaxed, breathing deeply and almost touching it with outstretched fingers. At the same time, he began to shower the plant with the same type of affectionate emotion he would flow to a friend. Each time he did this, a series of ascending oscillations was described on the [galvanometer's] chart by the pen holder. At the same time Vogel could tangibly feel, on the palms of his hands, an outpouring from the plant of some sort of energy."[4]

In another experiment, Vogel connected two plants to the same galvanometer and snipped a leaf from the *first* plant to observe the following:

*"The **second** plant responded to the hurt being inflicted on its neighbor, but **only** when Vogel **was paying attention to it!** If Vogel cut a leaf while ignoring the second plant, the response was lacking."*

As you go about your own plant experiment, within a few days the plant will begin to improve and flourish. And don't be surprised when it does. You'll know the truth behind the mystery. This phenomenon will have occurred not because of you talking to the plant, or playing soft music, but merely because you *paid attention* to the plant. You, and the plant, have shared Life force – the aspect linking everything to God.

When you see this, it will be one of those "duh... that's a no-brainer" moments for you.

Do we not feel better and healthier when we are surrounded by friends (instead of non-partisan strangers)? Do we not feel better when a friend comes to us and says: "Hey, is everything okay? I just wanted to say *I care*."

On the other side, do we not feel better when we check up on a friend? When we go to them and say: "Hey, is everything okay? You doing all right?"

Of course we do. And like animals and people – plants are living things too. They respond the same.

In other words, after a week of visiting the plant twice daily, not only will the plant feel better, but you'll feel better too.

As another mention, studies have shown that people with pets often recover faster from illnesses.

Do you see the link?

Love – appreciation and care– is a form of energy. It is a tool.

The Second Law of the Universe is this:

Whenever we openly share our life force with another creature – be that a human or a cat or a plant or an infant in the womb – our own life force *grows*, as does the life force of those we are helping (or who are helping us).

So how do we turn this switch "on" to share life force?

The answer is so elementary it may astound you: through *sincere appreciation.*

Whenever we act with love, with each act of kindness, we open the doorways to divinity and creation. Whenever we act with

25

fear, however, we slam these doorways shut.

Love opens all channels, while fear closes them down. Love facilitates sharing, while fear demands selfishness. Love allows us to be exposed, while fear insists we be covered. Love provides unconditional acceptance, while fear stipulates requirements. Love enables abundance. Fear chases abundance away.

"There is no fear in love; but rather love casteth out fear: because fear hath torment. He that feareth is not made perfect in love."
1 John 4:19
The Bible
KJV

By appreciating every living being that we encounter, we initiate the exchange of life force.

If you do the "plant experiment", you'll see firsthand evidence of the law of shared energy. But there are other signs to follow. God has given us *many* ways of finding this truth. We can feel it inside, and we can see it through subtle evidence in life.

If we look at a pair of lovers (such as those in the Parable of the Lovers) we can witness the phenomenon firsthand. We see them full of life, buoyant, and feeling on top of the world. We notice the "glow" on their faces.

Think about the last time you were with a person and you really felt "connected" with that person. Like the young couple in the mall, the two of you were being open and sharing. Your face may have been "aglow" without your realizing such. You may have felt a certain sense of "vulnerability" at the time, because of dropping your defenses; yet you felt comfortable enough with that person to allow them "inside".

Without realizing it, you were openly sharing your life force with that person. And whenever we share our life force, it grows.

*For where two or three are gathered in my name, there am I **in the midst of them**.*

St. Matthew 18: 20
The Bible
KJV

While it's often easiest to share our life force with a loved one, a trusted friend, or a family member, love is *not* a pre-requisite. This energy-sharing phenomenon can occur between absolute strangers.

Have you ever sat down next to a perfect stranger, engaged in some small talk, and the next thing you know you're discussing intimate or personal information that you haven't even confided to your most trusted friends? (A common example of this may be the fellow who goes into a bar and tells his woes to the bartender).

In the situation of strangers, unless we intuitively feel threatened by a gesture or some other sign, we gradually drop our life force "guard" as we interact with the stranger. The longer the conversation continues without threat, the lower our guard falls. We do this because we inherently *want* – we long – to connect and share life force. And once both parties have dropped this guard and "bonded", openly sharing life force, the life force can "flow and grow".

27

This phenomenon is not limited to human strangers, and can also be applied to our interactions with animals. Have you ever noticed how, if you are afraid of a certain animal, that animal can sense your fear?

Here's another angle to consider (and there are literally hundreds):

How many times have you heard it said "the bride looked radiant"?

Are brides not showered with attention?

By the same token, if a single coworker comes into work one morning with a certain "glow", we might think: *"Wow. They must have met someone."* or *"Wow. They got lucky last night..."*. (Sex can be a powerful exchange of Life force energy – a virtual merging, and cause the glow).

Or also consider this:

How do you *feel* when someone pays you a sincere compliment? Or better yet, try paying someone a compliment and see if you don't feel better afterwards.... (You will, because you are *appreciating* and sharing life force; as a result, *your own life force grows*).

Try it today. What do you have to lose?

When it comes to compliments, we sometimes find ourselves *afraid* (*fear*ing) to *pay* a compliment because it feels like we are giving away a part of our self. In effect, you can now see that we *are* "giving something up", and therefore have had valid reasons for this mysterious feeling. The next step of ascension is realizing that God replaces what we "forfeit" with *more of what we had.*   Whenever you sincerely appreciate someone (or something), and share your life force, *your own life force grows.*   In other words, by helping others you're helping yourself.

But most of us don't need to see this phenomenon to know it. We know it from our own experiences.   At the height of being in love, when we're still in that "new romance" stage, we wake up each morning full of life (instead of groggy), anxious to see that special person.   And when we're with them, life couldn't be better.   When separated from that person, if only for a few hours, we suddenly feel very alone and perhaps even "down".

When we're with the special someone – that new "light of our life" – we're openly sharing energy.   And as we share our energy, admire them, pay compliments freely, our own Life force grows.   We then feel "alive" and "vibrant".

The following poem might demonstrate how the author sensed this occurrence and tried to capture it in words:

> *...when our gazes meet, and you smile,*
> *my soul is drawn through my eyes,*
> *like the morning mist on a dark sea*
> *it rises toward the skies.*

> *A.M.H.*

This is the lesson we must learn in order to mature as a spiritual presence.

As another example of "energy at work", we need only observe pregnant women.   Like a bride glowing, how many times have you seen a pregnant woman seem to "glow"? Logic – Mankind's

29

flawed foundation of thinking – would dictate that a pregnant woman should look tired and worn out. After all, she's feeding two (or more). Her body is going through a host of chemical changes. She may be struggling with bouts of morning sickness, cramps that prevent sleep, and she may be carrying an extra 20 or 30 pounds around the clock! Based on "logic", a mother-to-be *should look like she's on her death bed!* You would expect her to have hollow and sunken eyes and pallid skin. Certainly, you wouldn't expect her to glow.

The explanation, again, is quite simple. For one, a pregnant woman receives lots of positive, *caring* attention. And secondly, she is sharing her life force with the fetus, and *caring* about the fetus.

Celebrities are yet another example of this phenomenon. When you see celebrities on TV (or performing), they almost always look good. Even when a reporter catches them off guard, they look vibrant and full of life; often look years younger than their true age.

We say *"she can stay looking that young because she leads such a pampered life"* or *"she's probably had a dozen tummy-tucks and 5 face-lifts"* (which may be true in some cases) or *"she's got to be wearing pancake makeup!"* But now that you know the underlying mechanics, the answer should be clear. Think of all the attention celebrities receive! Why do you think so many of us *long to be celebrities* in one shape or form? The money is great, but is that the primary reason?

Isn't it the *attention?*

And if so, *why* do we *crave* that attention? Do we really want media personnel hiding in our shrubbery and waiting for us every time we leave our home?

Do we ever want anyone to say a bad (negative) thing about us?

Of course not. We crave *money* and *power* (so that we can get *attention)* but what we most want is *positive attention*. Even if we're "shy", and don't want to bask in it, we still long to have people "oohing and ahhing" over us.

We crave attention, just as we crave food when hungry.

Think about it...

Here's one other presentation of this phenomenon that might lend a different type of insight:

Consider a thunderstorm. The more a thunderstorm grows, the more lightning (energy) it produces. As long as the storm is *growing*, it continues to both produce and discharge lightning. Only when the storm *stops growing* does the lightning begin to dissipate and bleed off.

A hurricane is yet another example. The more it grows, the more wind and rain (forms of energy) it produces.

Our own Divinity energy works on the same principle. Whenever we are growing and "share" our energy, we continue to *create* energy. When we stop growing or try to hoard our energy (due to *fears*), our energy begins to dissipate.

Children are another "in open sight" example for us. While a child is growing – especially during "growth spurts", they have seemingly boundless energy.

31

This whole process defies what we call "logic", because our foundation of thinking is based on humankind's erroneous perceptions of "limited supply" and "conservation". We become confused by "logic" because we think of this energy like a common battery: the more we use it, the shorter its life. But in reality the exact *opposite* is true. The more we use it, the *longer* and *fuller* its life.

Do people who exercise frequently and expend their energy live longer or shorter?

We crave "attention" so we can "recharge". The problem is, however, that we don't realize that getting "attention" is a mere substitute. (Yet we'll go to any means to get this attention). We can produce our own energy by *giving* it to others. We can also produce our own energy by staying active, and *by connecting with God*.

God is an infinite supply.

> ***Give, and it shall be given unto you***; *good measure, pressed down, and shaken together, and running over,* ***shall men give unto your bosom***. *For with the same measure that ye mete withal, it shall be measured to you again.*
>
> *St. Luke 6: 38*
> *The Bible*
> *KJV*

The next time you find yourself feeling low on energy – in that familiar couch-potato-mode in front of the TV – try taking a short walk through the local park. By doing so, you'll get a quick energy recharge. Whenever we are active, we produce energy. And better yet, whenever we visit Nature and *appreciate* Nature's beauty, we become attuned to God and are connected to the ultimate source.

Take time to enjoy and appreciate the *simplicities* of life.

Is getting the next load of laundry done so important that you can't take a moment to enjoy the sunset?

Take a moment to savor the fragrance of roses. Listen to the wind's sigh as it passes through the trees. Feel the caress of the sun on your skin. Look for a four-leaf clover.

Live!

By the time you return from that walk, you may be surprised by how much better you feel.

Again, love enables abundance; fear chases abundance away.

Chapter 5
Life Force Thieves

Just as we can share our life force energy, we can also steal it. And in turn, it can be stolen from us. Our own survival instincts teach us to guard our own supply, and steal when we "need". Because of this, we spend much of our lives playing "mind games" and competing for Life force, without ever realizing exactly what's happening behind the scenes.

To protect our life force, we each have an invisible "shield" (as we'll call it here). This shield is part of our "aura" (the fields of energy surrounding our physical body) and resides about 3-6 inches outside of our physical (and visible) body. It can be "dropped" when we choose to share life force, or "raised" to encapsulate us when we feel threatened. During routine matters, we normally hold our shield at "half-mast", lowering it only when we need to "consume", and raising it only when we need to protect our life force from being stolen.

When another person threatens to steal our life force, we unconsciously pick up signals and gestures from that person (we'll look closer at this later) and begin to raise our shield.

35

As an example most people can relate to, imagine that you're engaged in a conversation with two friends (or colleagues), and another person walks up and "steps inside your personal space" while joining in the conversation. When this occurs, we feel an indefinable encroachment caused by that person's "standing too close". Even if we are on friendly terms with that person, we often find ourselves taking a step back, avoiding eye contact, crossing our arms over our chest, steepling our fingers in front of us (if seated), or resting our chin in our palm – any method that supplements our shield, protecting our life force. Without explanation, our chest and face feels "vulnerable" and thus we try to cover them.

While there is no physical reason for our feeling "invaded" or "vulnerable" when someone "stands too close", there is a very valid spiritual reason. In effect, by penetrating our aura with theirs, they are creating a connection – a spiritual rape of sorts – that allows them to plunder your life force through intimidation. (More on this shortly).

As mentioned in James Redfield's The Celestine Prophecy[5], (a book I'd highly recommend), there are four basic "control dramas" we all use to steal Life force. The first of these covers intimidation.

I've expanded these "control dramas" here into what I term "Personality Modes". I've also added two new ones (which will be discussed in a later chapter).

For the moment, however, we'll focus on the basic four so you can learn about them and can watch people around you use them. You'll want to learn about these personality modes (PMs) because – through them – people steal our Life force. As a matter of fact, we each have used one (or more) of these personality modes to steal Life force when we need it. We adopt PMs as children, and can switch among them as each situation warrants.

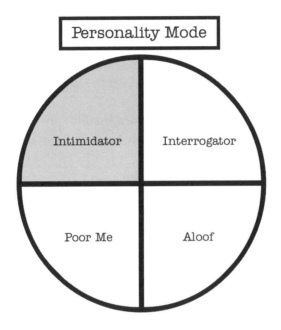

Personality Mode

Intimidator | Interrogator

Poor Me | Aloof

1. THE INTIMIDATOR:

Of the four personality modes (PMs), the first we'll discuss is "The Intimidator".

The Intimidator acquires life force from other individuals by either "intimidating" them or "breaking their spirit" to make them pay attention. Intimidators are commonly male, use fear as their tool, and often marry "Poor Mes" (discussed shortly).

Intimidators are often large and imposing, loud-spoken, aggresive, and competitive. They are quick to yell, and quick to pick a fight. They are often arrogant, with a "Me First" attitude. They attempt to control, and have violent proclivities. Intimidators sometimes display unexpected outbursts and always strive to hold "center stage". They tend to order others around and try to maintain as aura of power and authority. They are egocentric, like stare-downs, and have an unpleasant habit of 'standing too close".

If you enjoy profiling, the Intimidator is often the "Middle Child" of a family. Being neither the oldest nor the youngest, they have to "make noise" to be noticed and get the attention they need.

By this same token, people who are small in physical stature are sometimes (surprisingly) Intimidators. Again, this is because they must "make noise" to be noticed.

In high school, Intimidators are often the "Jocks" and are also the "bullies". In adult life, they are often in authoritative roles, such as corporate management or law.

Their favorite words are: "Do 'x' for me".

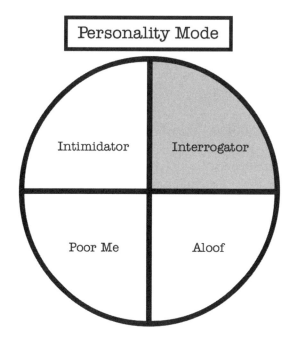

Personality Mode

Intimidator | Interrogator

Poor Me | Aloof

2. THE INTERROGATOR:

Interrogators are less physically threatening than Intimidators, and "break the spirit" of others by questioning every action and motive, placing them on the defensive, and/or by dominating a conversation through a string of questions. They "control" by keeping people under their scrutiny.

When the Intimidator has an unexpected outburst, the Interrogator will be the first person in the room to stand up and say: "Why'd you do that? That was uncalled for! What was your reasoning?", launching a series of questions designed to put the Intimidator in a defensive posture.

Interrogators are often the oldest child of a family. As adults, they may be teachers, attorneys, counselors, reporters, or hold other positions which involve probing or instructing. They can be either male or female, but more often than not, they are female.

They often have a fear of being deserted or betrayed, due to a desertion that happened at a young age. They are typically cynical of the world, and thus evolve into the role of Interrogator – questioning every motive.

Their favorite word is: "Why?"

Of the four basic personality types, the Interrogator is the highest evolved and the most in touch with receiving natural energy (through friendly conversations). The Intimidator and the Poor Me battle for the lowest position, with the "Aloof" falling in the middle.

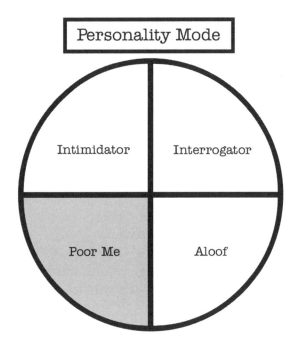

3. THE POOR ME:

The Poor Me gains attention by eliciting pity. Their goal is to make you feel sorry for them so you will listen (and pay them attention). They draw attention to themselves by sighing, crying, looking worried, and retelling their unfortunate plights and hardships in exquisite and often exaggerated detail. They love to gossip and "stir the pot of controversy", thriving when they are in the midst of a crisis or drama.

They are sometimes perpetually "ill" and constantly need help in one form or another – be that health, money, or emotional support.

When help is offered to a Poor Me however, it is often rejected ("Thanks... but that won't help because of ..."). Instead, when a method for resolve is offered, the Poor Me plays up the problem as "irresolvable" and will strive to keep the problem alive. This is because if the conflict at hand is resolved, the Poor Me will no longer be a "victim", thus ending their means of receiving attention.

The Poor Me is usually female and is often a middle or next-to-the-youngest child. As adults, they may be "kept" women or hold low-income jobs. They can also be the "over-worked and underpaid person that no one sees". They frequently call in sick from their job, and have difficulty succeeding in the workplace. They often complain of their illnesses while at work. (Which, again, makes them a victim).

The Poor Me's favorite word is: "But..."

The Poor Me can go into an "Aloof" mode, whereas they fall into a funk of self-pity. They immediately return to "Poor Me" when someone notices their despair. ("All these terrible things happened – this, and that, and this – and I was so hurt by all these things, and then no one paid attention, which made it even worse!").

An Intimidator is drawn to a Poor Me when the Poor Me needs a "savior" or "hero". Once these two get together, they begin a cycle that may escalate to physical violence over time. The Intimidator can easily dominate and control the Poor Me, thus stealing the Poor Me's energy. In turn, when the Intimidator pushes too far, the Poor Me goes into a crying, "victim" mode until the Intimidator apologizes and "pays back" the attention, thus completing the cycle.

The Intimidator/Poor Me relationship is the classic master/slave. It can also be the classic "caregiver/receiver" relationship.

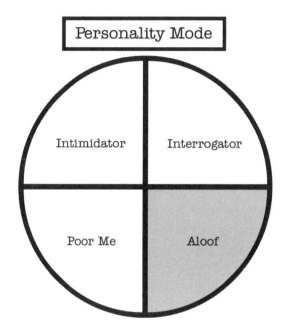

4. ALOOF:

The Aloof are very passive and tend to walk away from confrontation. They are quiet and introspective, need a lot of space, and don't like being pinned down by commitments. They are loners by default, and can be uncooperative, condescending, and very analytical. They usually have many self-doubts, and are quick to become defensive. They have difficulty making up their minds, taking any particular stance, and saying "no".

Their favorite phrase is: "It doesn't matter".

They get their energy by being detached, unaffected, or mysterious so that others will try to "draw them out".

The Aloof are often the "only child", may be of either sex, but are most frequently males. As adults, they prefer jobs which provide privacy, a low risk of confrontation, and/or a low amount of commitment.

The Aloof and the Interrogator are often drawn together when the Interrogator approaches the Aloof and does an "interview".

Problems can occur when the Aloof becomes too secretive, or the Interrogator over-scrutinizes.

Chapter 6
Development of Personality Modes

Okay. Did you get a basic glimpse of the four major Personality Modes (PMs)?

Did reading through the PM descriptions cause a face to come to mind? An old boyfriend or girlfriend/ Mom or dad? Your boss?

If you could put faces with the PMs, and could recognize the major traits in people you know, great for you. The better you understand the PMs, the faster you'll be able to recognize a PM when another person tries to use it against you. The faster you can recognize it, the easier it is to throw up roadblocks.

"But when would someone use a PM? And why would they use it?"

We use PMs to "get the things we want". Whether the "thing" is a physical item, attention, or just "the upper hand" in a given situation, we use PMs as a tool to help us acquire.

If you're the parent of a 3-8 year old child, over the course of time you will observe your child testing the four basic personality modes to learn the effectiveness of each one as their tool. As children, we have each done this. Once we've found one that works well or fits, we wear it like a second skin. Under certain situations, however, we can temporarily assume another personality mode when the need arises. This is akin to carrying a "major" and "minor" in college. For example, if one Intimidator is confronted by a more powerful Intimidator, the less powerful Intimidator may become Aloof or a Poor Me.

If you're a parent, you should be able to relate with the upcoming descriptions of a child's "personality mode testing process". If you're not yet a parent, you can easily observe the "testing" process by visiting a local grocery store, especially those that have gum ball machines near the entrance. As it is, I suspect these machines are encoded with subliminal messages that only children can interpret or hear. The messages infallibly cause any passerby child to beg for change; a shrewd marketing campaign on the part of the machine makers.

When the first child comes through the supermarket doors, asks for change, and is told a stern "No" by the parent, get out your notepad and get ready for the action...

Testing the Poor Me Mode:

With very few exceptions, most children will test the "Poor Me" continuum first. They begin this test by "begging" once they've been told "no" ("Pleeeeease... I'll be real good."). If they're told "no!" a second time, the child typically begins to cry, and may bawl at an embarrassing volume well after entering the store. They elicit pity by saying things such as: "You don't love me." "Nobody loves me." "My stomach hurts because I'm so hungry (even though they've just eaten)" or "Johnny always gets one and I never do." (Etc., etc.).

We've all seen it and know the signs.

When the child realizes the Poor Me approach isn't working (it may take them several tries), they climb to the next level: Intimidator mode.

Testing the Intimidator Mode:

In Intimidator mode, the child becomes loud and sometimes even violent. They often yell phrases such as: "I don't like you anymore!" Or "I hate you!" Or "You've GOT to give me a quarter! Give it to me! If you don't, I'll tell Dad!" Or even "I'll break something if you don't! I'll hit you if you don't!" (Etc).

Again, we've all seen it and know it can be ugly.

Testing the Aloof Mode:

If the Intimidator mode fails, the next progression is Aloof mode. This occurs when the angry child, realizing the Intimidator mode is failing, either runs away to hide or goes mute and refuses to speak. We often term this as "bulling" or "pouting". In some cases, at this point of the spectrum, a parent may say something like: "If you're good through the rest of the store, I'll give you a quarter and you can get a gum ball as we leave." And invariably, the next time the situation repeats itself, the child will rapidly progress to the Aloof mode because they know it works. If, however, the child bulls and is told: "You can keep bulling if you want, but you're NOT getting a quarter!", the child will likely move to the next level.

Testing the Interrogator Mode:

After failing with the Poor Me, the Intimidator, and the Aloof, some children (but not all) will progress to the Interrogator mode. This is when the child begins asking (with a mix of sincerity and scrutiny): "Why can't I have it? Why don't you want me to have

47

it? What's wrong with sugar? Why is sugar bad for you? Why don't you have enough money?" (Etc., Etc.).

At this point, the child has made the complete cycle. They've hurled all their ammo at you, and their only choice is to try to comprehend your rationale for not buying them that coveted gum ball.

The lesser degrees of PMs:

Thus far, we've looked at the four personality modes in their extremes. By knowing the predominant traits and characteristics of each PM, you ease the identification process.

In actuality, however, most people fall on a scale from mild to extreme within their chosen personality mode. Thus, finding a textbook example is a rarity.

Within the four "parent" modes, there are also numerous "sub-personality modes". While we need not hamper our learning by discussing each of these individual subs, let me present two brief examples.

As one, many of us may know a "Dreamer" (some would call this person a "BS'er", but I prefer the kinder term). The Dreamer is a sub-personality mode of Interrogator. That is, rather than outwardly "question and interrogate", a Dreamer "commands attention" by telling people all the great things he/she is going to do (or has supposedly already accomplished).

A second example might be the "Know-it-all". The Know-it-all "rides the fence" between Interrogator and Intimidator by fishing for information with questions, then dominating a conversation with their "wide and comprehensive knowledge" of the topic at hand. Being a "fence rider", we might equate the Know-it-all to the color "teal", being neither green nor blue, but somewhere in between. And just as teal looks more blue when surrounded by green, or green when surrounded by blue, the Know-it-all can assume the stance of Intimidator (when surrounded by Interrogators) or Interrogator (when dealing with Intimidators).

Can a PM be used positively? And if not, why?

What's important to understand is, PMs are like the ski-mask to the robber. They hide our True Self and are used to manipulate situations and otherwise steal or commandeer life force.

When our life force dips low, and we feel compelled to steal, we reach in our spiritual backpack and select the most appropriate PM "ski-mask" for the crime. After going about the dastardly deed, we remove the mask, and return to Who We Really Are.

Because the act of assuming a PM is a denial of our True Self, it is negative by default. It is a tacit statement that: "we cannot be happy, nor receive enough attention, being Who We Really Are... therefore, we must steal to survive". Reverting to the use of a PM also denies that God can – and will – fulfill our every "need".

In the highest sense, the "need" to use a PM is a consequence of spiritual transgressions. When we give in to fear-based sins (i.e. pride, selfishness, lust, etc.) rather than treating others with love, we inadvertently block ourselves from receiving life force that we would have received, had we acted with love. This then creates a shortage of life force, and compels us to steal from others.

To make matters worse, we then cause ourselves additional spiritual hardship by scratching and clawing at our spiritual siblings, fighting over a dime's worth of life force, while God stands by offering free dollars to anyone who will accept.

(We'll discuss fear-based sins in more detail later).

Because using a PM is a self-denial, it is always a negative act with negative consequences. The degree of negativity may be lessened, however, if a PM is used in a positive manner (out of genuine concern for another individual). For example, in the following illustration (which would apply to many families), the mother figure is shown as an Interrogator. Although the mother is depicted here as an Interrogator, this does not mean she constantly interrogates members of the family. It may be that she only dons the Interrogator PM during family arguments, or as a mode of self-defense. It may also be that she is a very loving and caring individual, and acquires life force through the correct channels of appreciation. Perhaps she has a "Poor Me" acquaintance she calls or visits during the day, thus freely giving (and receiving) life force by showing concern about the Poor Me's "never-ending hardships and problems". It may also be that the mother uses her Interrogator traits as a tool to find thrifty purchases, protect the family from scams, or for otherwise probing.

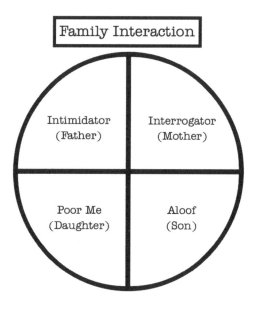

Assuming no member of the family is extreme in their **PM** and acquires their life force from outside the family, the above illustration is the classic model of a functional family. In this model, with all members of the family holding a different **PM**, there is an equal balance. When any given family member feels forced to steal life force from within the family structure, they can use their own unique **PM** to acquire it. Likewise, the target of such theft can use their own unique **PM** as an aid for self-protection, and/or to re-acquire stolen life force.

As an example, using the previous illustration, let's assume that the father (an Inimidator) has a particularly bad at work. Let's assume that when the father arrives at work, his boss (a more powerful Intimidator) presents a list of tasks, demanding the tasks be completed by the end of the day. As the father goes about his work, trying to accomplish these tasks, a lateral colleague (an Interrogator) constantly interrupts, inquiring about the progress of the projects. In the meantime, a subordinate employee (a Poor Me) calls in late because of "not feeling well", then mopes around after arriving, complaining of how badly he or she feels (instead of getting needed tasks accomplished).

In a case such as this, all three of the father's co-workers have used their PMs to leech away at the father's life force throughout the day. Thus, by the time the father arrives home, he feels emotionally abused and "drained". Unknowingly, he is starved for life force. Yet not understanding how life force works, the father equates his grouchy and "uneasy" mood to "the bad day". In situations such as this, we often "strike out" at those around us without just reason.

Why?

The problem is like a two-sided coin. On one side, we are trying to recover lost life force; on the other, we are trying to rid ourselves of fear (as we'll discuss later), and cast fears onto others.

For our purposes here, we'll assume that when the father arrives home, he "snaps" at his teenage son (an Aloof) for not mowing the grass.

Why again?

Without understanding the underlying mechanics, the father feels compelled to intimidate someone and make their day as miserable as his. What he doesn't understand is, he is desperate to steal life force.

If you are beginning to grasp how the PMs work, you can virtually predict the scene that's about to play out with this family. The moment the father dons his Intimidator mask, the whole family subconsciously senses it, and dons masks of their own.

1. The son (Aloof), stomps out of the room, grumbling to himself while heading for his bedroom.
2. The father (Intimidator), follows the son, demanding the son stop and listen. ("I pay the bills here and keep a roof over your head and food on your plate. The least you can do is a simple thing like mow the yard when I tell you!")
3. The mother (Interrogator), follows on the father's heels. ("Do you have to start on him the moment you walk in the door?")
4. The teenage daughter (Poor Me), immediately begins to cry and phones a friend to tell them about the terrible fight her parents and brother are having.

As you can see here, a single use of a PM can cause a chain reaction.

The ultimate challenge to learn is:

We need never rely on any PM to acquire life force or to be "happy".

At any time, we can acquire life force freely and abundantly by merely appreciating an individual (or being) for who (or what) they are, and addressing their fears and concerns with love and respect.

So how could this needless family squabble have been avoided?

Suppose for a moment that when the father arrived home, he took a deep breath and paused for a moment to silently appreciate his home and his family. Suppose that he paused to thank God for giving him a home to come home to (despite the tall grass, it provided warmth and shelter). And suppose he thanked God for providing him with a loving wife (at home, waiting to greet him). And that his teenage son was at home (instead of out dealing drugs, in trouble with the law, or otherwise carousing). And that his teenage daughter was also home and healthy (instead of drug dependent, pregnant, etc.).

53

As you can see, through appreciation (love), we can quickly "recharge" our life force while also ridding ourselves of fear. The process of prevention begins with each of us, and is accomplished in three simple steps;

1. First, and perhaps most difficult, we must learn to recognize whichever **PM** we tend to use when we "seek attention" or try to "get the upper hand" during power struggles. Do we become Intimidators? Do we become Aloof? Do we become Interrogators? Seek Pity? Use some "blend" in between?

   By understanding our own chosen **PM** and its characteristics, we can learn to recognize when we "don the **PM** mask", and then how to stop ourselves from being "Aloof", "Interrogating", (etc.), thus "removing the **PM** mask" and stepping outside the **PM** circle.

2. Second, we must learn to identify the **PM**s other people use. In doing so, we guard ourselves from being manipulated, and allow ourselves to move on to step three.

3. Third, and most important, we can help others remove their own masks... even when they don't realize they're wearing them.

How?

Again, this occurs through appreciation. It begins by appreciating the person using the **PM** for Who They Truly Are, instead of focusing on their present (unbecoming) behavior.

Next, it continues by freely giving that person our attention.

Why?

Again, whenever we share our life force – give our attention – our own life force grows.

And finally, as we will discuss shortly, every hardship, or crisis, or struggle – every "negative" is in collusion with FEAR.

Love, however, overcomes.

As we move to the next section, consider these:

And thou shalt love the Lord thy God with all thy heart, and with all thy soul, and with all thy mind, and with all thy strength: this [is] the first commandment.
And the second [is] like, [namely] this, Thou shalt love thy neighbour as thyself. There is none other commandment greater than these.
Mark 12:30-31
The Bible
KJV

Give and it shall be given unto you; good measure, pressed down, and shaken together, and running over, shall men give into your bosom. For with the same measure that ye mete withal it shall be measured to you again.
Luke 6:38
The Bible
KJV

"And if any man will sue thee at the law, and take away thy coat, let him have thy cloak also. And whosoever shall compel thee to go a mile, go with him twain (two)."
"But I say unto you, Love your enemies, bless them that curse you, do good to them that hate you, and pray for them which despitefully use you, and prosecute you."
Matthew 5:40-41, 44
The Bible
KJV

55

Chapter 7
We all have Spiritual Needs

Okay. Time to change subjects so we can leap forward.

To maintain good emotional health, we each have certain "needs" which must be fulfilled to balance our lives (see figure below).

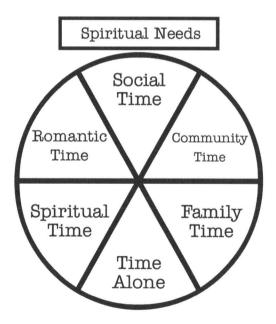

As one example, most people can relate to needing "Time Alone", which is one of the six primary emotional needs. Having "time alone" gives us a chance to merely reflect, to wind down, plan for the future, or escape the pressures of everyday life.

At other times, we need "Social Time" to get out-and-about and laugh with colleagues, peers, and friends. We also need "Romantic Time" with our mate; that time bonding with our life partner.

"Family Time" is another of our needs; having the safe-haven of family where we can be around loved ones, share concerns, and feel we have a place in the world where we "belong".

"Community Time" is yet another; it makes us feel we're doing "our part" to help our local community. For some people, fulfilling "Community Time" may be done by volunteering to help an organization, by contributing to charity, or it may be as simple as recycling plastics and paper.

Beyond these other needs, we also need "Spiritual Time". Regardless of the God (or Goddess) you worship – be that Allah, Buddha, Diana, Elohim, God, Jehovah, Yahweh or another deity – we all need time to commune and pay reverence to our Creator. The problem is, while most people recognize their other needs (such as time alone or social needs), many don't feel they have any spiritual needs. If you walk the streets and ask passersby if they have "spiritual needs", I think you'll be astounded by how many people answer "no" or "very little".

But I'd like to pose a thought for you to ponder...

"It's not that people don't have spiritual needs – they do – it's merely a problem of their religion not doing anything for them (at least not anything tangible or readily visible)."

We'll refer back to our "Farm Parable" for some insight into people not recognizing their own spiritual needs. If, before they entered the hen house, Johnny's father had suggested that Johnny study multiplication tables, Johnny would have likely balked at the idea. And with good reason, because he couldn't yet comprehend the value of spending many hours learning to multiply. At that moment in his life, as they walked toward the hen house door, multiplication held no value for Johnny because it doesn't do anything for you.

Some people view spiritual needs the same. They view religion as "not doing anything for you". In example, for the first 25 years of his life "Jim Doe" may have attended church but gained nothing "tangible" from it. Jim might recognize that during those 25 years, the church taught him good moral values, helped instill his ethical standards, and taught a great deal about the Bible. It also provided him with a forum to quench his "Social Needs". And by "being a good citizen", attending church each week, tithing part of his earnings, and volunteering for roles within the church (Deacon, Sunday School Teacher, the Choir, etc.), his participation with the church also helped to fulfill his "Community Needs". But because his spiritual needs were unfulfilled, at age 26 Jim determined "he had no spiritual needs".

Learning multiplication was doing nothing for him.

The problem with many forms of organized religion is a fundamental one, paved with good intentions, but governed by flawed principles. Jim expected the hours he was at church − those hours he had set aside from his busy, hectic life − to help him feel closer to God. The Church, on the other hand, viewed its role as a fellowship and "classroom" environment, expecting the individual to learn about God while there, but to set aside other hours of their life for the actual communing.

As you can see, this scenario creates a likely conflict and outcome. People such as Jim often pass through life being active members of a church (for months and even years) only to "drop out" and later return. They sense they are getting "something" they need from the church (the fulfillment of their social/community needs), yet also feel they're not finding what they sought (a connection with God).

With that said, if you attend a church and observe this problem, you can initiate a remedy by helping others realize the problem exists. Identifying the problem is the difficult part of the equation. Once the problem is acknowledged, solving it is simple. In this case, you might suggest that the church incorporate one night per week which has no "service" and focuses on individuals merely communing with God.

While we're on the subject of organized religion, I will point out one downfall of many belief systems. Many belief systems are based on fear instead of Love. Whenever we fear, we immediately erect our Life force shield and block the sharing of energy. Only when we love – appreciate or care – can we share energy.

We go to church seeking spiritual solace with our God, and leave feeling "the fear of God". We are taught never to judge – yet learn that God is (supposedly) judgmental and will judge us and swiftly determine how we spend eternity. We are instructed never to anger or seek revenge – wrath is the Lord's – and all the while, TV talk show psychologists tell us : "it's okay to feel anger".

Is it no shock we are confused?

I tell you now that God does not want you to live in confusion or fear.

Ever.

Would you wish such on your own children?

God wants you to be happy.

You're currently on the path. Read on.

Chapter 8
The Interaction of Life Force and Our Emotional Needs

Okay. In this section we get to connect the first two "puzzle-piece islands" and gain an important insight into life's puzzle.

As I mentioned earlier, our level of available life force can change from day-to-day, even hour-to-hour, and directly impacts our outlook on life.

Our life force level also works in close conjunction with our emotional needs.

Balanced Life Force & Emotional Needs

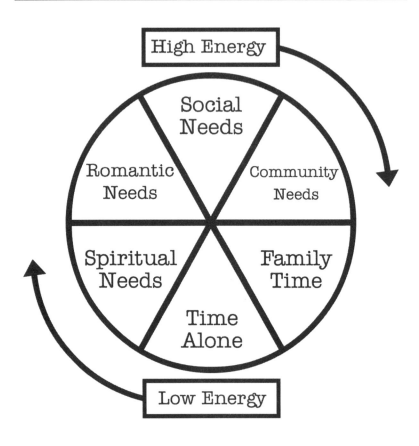

TIMES OF LOW LIFE FORCE ENERGY:

When our life force energy dips critically low in supply, our "Time Alone" need increases. And during these shortages we often sleep or relax to refresh our life force.

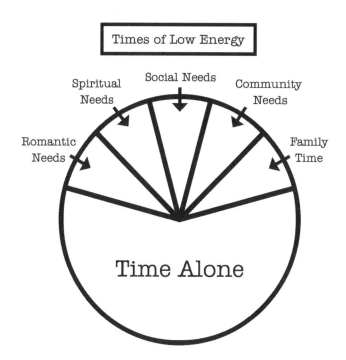

Through personal observation we can see that chronic shortages of life force are directly related — if not responsible — for the disease we call clinical depression. In the case of people who are clinically depressed, the "Time Alone" need grows out of proportion until it consumes three-quarters (or more) of the pie, thus scrunching the other five needs into small slivers. In other words, people who suffer from critical life force shortages are so (unknowingly) desperate to restore their life force, they begin exhibiting the classic symptoms of depression. That is:

1. They often "hole up" and spend a great deal of time sleeping. (Trying to refresh life force).
2. Suddenly lose interest in hobbies and pursuits they formerly enjoyed. (Activities which may have previously fulfilled their social, romantic, spiritual, family, or community needs).
3. Have difficulty concentrating or thinking clearly. (The "sparks" or "thoughts" [energy] have difficulty "arcing" between neuron-transmitters in the brain).
4. They complain of lacking "energy" or motivation.
5. Feel "lifeless" and have suicidal thoughts.

In some cases involving the clinically depressed, it may be that a person around them is "stealing" or draining their life force and thus perpetuating the life force shortage. This most frequently occurs within the Intimidator/Poor Me relationship, with the Poor Me being the victim. Because of focusing on the negative aspects of most situations, and because of chronically being "ill", the Poor Me is already primed for major depression.

TIMES OF MODERATE LOWS:

In moderate life force shortages, we may refresh our life force through communing with God (spiritual needs). Or we may turn to family (family needs) where we can confide about problems, share life force, or even "steal" life force.

TIMES OF HIGH ENERGY:

When our life force energy is peaked – our internal battery at full charge – we feel jubilant and full of life. We are quick-witted and ready for action. Our emotions flow freely and we can barely stand to be alone. And during this time, our social needs soar because we need to be around others and "infect" them with our own enthusiasm for life. We feel like a cup overflowing. We have so much energy we need to spread it around or burn it off.

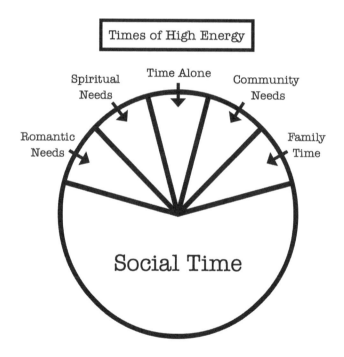

TIMES OF MODERATE HIGHS:

In moderate life force highs, we might fulfill our community needs by tackling a new project for the community or our job. Or we might fulfill our romantic needs by going out with a loved one.

Balancing our "Pie":

As you can imagine, there are virtually unlimited variations of the "Emotional Needs pie". In order to achieve a well-rounded and rewarding lifestyle, we must each strive to balance our own individual pie.

When I first considered including these "pies" here, I saw certain "pros" and "cons" resulting from their inclusion. The greatest "pro" was that the pies serve as a strong visual aid, conveying a point more fully and clearly than an equal amount of text. The biggest "con" was that the "pie graphs" present the erroneous perception that one must dedicate an equal amount of "time" to each "slice of pie". What's important to realize is, it's not the quantity of time we dedicate toward each need, but rather the quality of that time dedicated to each need. A good 30-minute heart-to-heart conversation with a family member can provide more fulfillment toward one's "family needs" than a full day in which you are merely together with a family member.

As we have seen, maintaining one's pie first begins with how they acquire life force. For example, if a person becomes "low on life force" and does not connect with God to restore, they may become depressed and thus are forced to use certain PMs and the "Time Alone" slice of the pie as an "inlet" or "source" for life force. As an end result, the person's life becomes unbalanced, bringing about certain hardships (we will explore shortly).

What's important to understand is, to maintain a true balance of our pie, our life force must be acquired from "within" – through love and appreciation – and then must be channeled "out" through the various "slices".

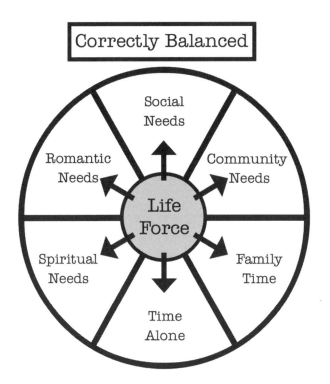

Chapter 9
Knowing "The Unknown"

Okay. We've assembled a few chunks of our life puzzle, yet the puzzle is still incomplete. Now, let's begin to broaden our view.

As we progress on our journey, there are two valuable lessons you will continue to notice along the way, that will be expanded upon much later:

1. All aspects of life are interconnected
2. All aspects of life occur in cycles.

In effect, life is like a divine gearbox, with one gear driving another, and the second gear driving yet another. There are gears that turn clockwise, causing others to turn counterclockwise. And even though two gears may be of different size, turning in different directions, if we look closely we can always find a connection.

As an example of this, we might refer back to how "life force" interplays with our "emotional needs". In effect, life force is but one universal gear that appears to stand completely alone. Similarly, our "emotional needs" appear to be yet another gear, also standing alone. If one takes a few steps back, however, and widens their view, they can see how these two gears have interlocking teeth, with one driving (or binding) the other.

71

Stepping back even further, one can see how "the gear of life force" not only drives the "gear of our emotional needs", but also drives other gears on its other sides, including one we'll call the "gear of The Unknown".

Long-Distance Life Force Exchanges:

To begin our exploration of "the gear of the unknown", it's important to realize that individuals need not be face-to-face for a life force exchange to take place. An exchange can occur at any given distance, regardless of the locality of either individual involved. It can happen during phone calls, radio conversations, or even in chat sessions online. Any exchange of life force can include the sharing, or stealing of life force.

Life force exchanges can also be completely one-sided. That is, as you'll see in some of the upcoming examples, we can freely send life force to another being by merely focusing our attention toward that being.

Online "Chat Room" affairs:

To launch our exploration of the "unknown", we'll first begin by looking at a topic that doesn't appear "other-worldly", yet strikes many people as a very "illogical" or "unexplainable" occurrence, and is directly related to our current topic.

If you stay abreast of the news, you've likely heard stories of the extramarital affairs being born every day in internet "chat rooms". For many people, it's difficult to understand how these "chat-room" affairs can occur.

After all, how logical is it to "fall in love" with someone you've never met? And how could someone leave a spouse of 10 or 20 years, for a basic stranger?

If you're one of the people who have difficulty fathoming these "blind romances", don't feel bad. More than one person has shook their head in disbelief. Through learning how life force exchanges occur, and by understanding how people crave life force (often without knowing it), you now should have an inkling of understanding.

When a spouse feels they aren't getting enough attention at home – or are "drained" by a spouse, they may go online with innocent and superficial intent of "meeting new friends". However – often unbeknownst to them – their underlying motive is to secure a new source of life force. Being starved for life force, they often feel drained and depressed. They may also feel an overwhelming sense of "restlessness". That is, they sense that "something is lacking" in their life, yet they are usually unsure what that "something" is. (Remember "Jim's" problem with church?).

You will recall from earlier lessons that: whenever we openly share our life force with another being, our own life force grows. This rule holds true in the case of chat-room interactions.

When two "life force-hungry" individuals meet in a chat room and begin sharing life force, their own energy begins to grow. The more they continue to share, the more their own energy grows. The more their energy grows, the better they begin to feel.

What has occurred is, the slice of their "emotional needs pie" called "romantic needs" has become the "inlet" or "source" for acquiring their life force. They are no longer acquiring life force from within – through their connection with God – but are instead connected to an outside source.

73

As a result of this increased life force they feel, they begin to attribute "feeling better and more full of life" to their chat relationship with "John" or "Jane". "Jane" or "John" has become their "God". Regardless of what is discussed, chatting with this person seems to make them "feel better" about themselves and brightens life in general. And since there's no other feasible explanation, they equate their "feeling better" – the "connection" they have with "John" or Jane" – to being in "love".

They often erroneously feel that due to the "connection" they feel, "John" or "Jane" is their "soul mate". They then may begin to feel they are "trapped in a marriage to the wrong spouse (because they have to "work" at that relationship)", and long to disconnect from their own life and spend all their time "connected" to this "soul mate". And even though these two people may be perfect strangers, from separate worlds and differing social circles or ethnic backgrounds, they will both be reluctant to cut themselves off from this new and vital source of life force.

Unknowingly, they become each other's primary source of life force and are increasingly dependent upon each other. Their real physical lives begin to take the second seat. The only remaining step is to meet with this "lover" in person so life force can be exchanged more directly.

You then have all the ingredients for a "consummated" affair.

If either individual is confronted by their spouse about their online relationship, they will often defend it with great tenacity. At some level of consciousness, they realize the online affair defies logic. They may also realize that this online "lover" is a basic stranger to them and the "lover" may have told them a host of lies which haven't been uncovered. Yet even facing that possibility, the individual will cling to the proverbial "thread of hope". They will make claims such as "they've really gotten to know the person" and go on about how this person is their "soul mate". Deep down, they may even know this "lover" isn't a good romantic or social match for them. However, rather than forfeit this crucial new source of positive life force, they will deny rationality and fight for the relationship – without truly understanding their own motives or the underlying mechanics.

If this unfortunate event has befallen someone you know, there is comfort through knowledge. By understanding how life force exchanges work, you can recognize and identify the underlying cause for infidelity. It isn't always a case of love ending, but is often a case of a spouse desperately seeking to fill an unfulfilled need.

If the relationship is still salvageable, I would strongly recommend marriage counseling and discussing life force exchanges with both parties – preferably by having them read this book and then openly discussing the content with them.

Psychometry and Imprinting:

Are things falling into place?

If so, great for you!

If not, be patient: good things come to those who wait.

To deepen our understanding of life force transmissions, especially those that transcend distant, let's look at one other analogy.

Suppose for a moment you were to sit down in front of a home CB radio station. By keying the microphone and speaking, your voice would be transmitted to any CB buffs who might be listening on the same channel. In return, these CB buffs could respond to anything you say; at which time you could converse with them, or could choose to ignore their comments.

Life force "transmissions" work in a very similar manner. The main difference is we don't need a "handle" and there's no equipment to buy. We don't need the slightest amount of technical savvy. God has made the process occur naturally. To choose a channel and broadcast, all we need to do is focus our attention at any given individual, group, animal, or even a stranger. Our base unit is always "powered up", and we never need to key the microphone, adjust the squelch, or tune the antenna. The "technical details" care for themselves.

Our emotions control the "signal strength" of any broadcast.

The stronger you feel at the moment of "transmit", the greater the life force energy you send. When the emotions are intense, an individual can hurl these "transmissions" around the globe. They can even reach into outer space and other dimensions – such as the afterlife.

This should help you understand why we feel "drained" after an intense situation, such as an argument. We find ourselves often needing to "cry on a shoulder" or be comforted (and thus recharge). Whether we "won" or "lost" the argument is usually irrelevant, as negative emotions – those based in fear – only serve to deplete life force.

This should also explain how you sometimes walk into a room and "sense tension in the air", even when the occupants are silent.

As a recipient of a life force transmission, you do not need to have the "sender" within your range of vision. Our subconscious has a built-in receiver – tools for detecting the transmission.

The "distance" between the two parties isn't determined by physical proximity, but instead by their emotional closeness and receptivity. In effect, the physical distance has very limited influence, if any at all.

In addition to spanning physical distances and realms, life force transmissions can also span time. This occurs through what we call "imprinting". When an item is infused with life force, it can serve as a "repository" for that life force long after events have taken place. Because both the item and the life force are made of energy, the life force can later be "tapped" or "extracted".

As an example to consider, let's assume that you sit down and write a handwritten letter. While you are composing the letter, because your attention is focused toward both the recipient and the letter, one "stream" of life force is hurled toward the recipient and another is sent toward the letter (which is a form of energy). The stream that is directed toward the letter is "absorbed" in the energy that makes up the letter. There, it becomes a resident.

If the sender's emotions are strong when writing the letter, the recipient may be able to "feel the emotion" that was "put into the letter" – days, weeks, or even years later.

By this same token, we can "imprint" any object.

As an example, we'll further explore this phenomenon by looking at the short story I've included below:

The Ring

In 1924, Frank Young decided to buy an engagement ring and propose to his lifelong sweetheart, Mary.

The problem Frank faced was, coming from a family of dirt-poor coal miners, there was no money for something as frivolous as jewelry, even for engagement.

Yet despite his poverty, Frank was determined to buy something very special for Mary.

To Frank, his relationship with Mary was priceless. It was born from the dust of poverty's coal, and was as persevering and sparkling as only one thing:

A diamond.

Nothing less would do.

Determined to get a special ring he had found at a local jewelers, Frank made a lay-away arrangement with the proprietor and took a second job black-smithing to pay for the ring.

Two years later, in late 1926, Frank paid off the ring and proposed to Mary.

Mary gleefully accepted.

To Mary, the fact that the ring bore a diamond was inconsequential. She would have gladly accepted his proposal had he picked up a rusty piece of wire and fashioned it into a ring. Coming from an equally poor family, Mary knew the sacrifice Frank had made to buy the ring, and that made the ring all the more sacred to her. It represented more than a mere marital token. It symbolized their love, non-ending; their relationship, perfect and scintillate; their promise. And their commitment.

In 1929, when Frank was sent to fight in World War I, Mary would often hold the ring whenever she missed Frank and worried of his safety.

As more years passed, after Frank had returned safely from the war, Mary would often hold the ring during any special moment. It was there at the birth of their first child, and there again, at the second. It was on her finger during their silver wedding anniversary, and there again during their golden. And even after Frank passed in 1986, the ring remained.

Although Mary could no longer bear to wear it.

It wasn't that the memories were too painful. Instead, because of the passage of time, and the increase in crimes against the elderly, she couldn't stand the thought of being robbed or mugged and allowing the ring — something so pure and sacred — to fall into unclean hands.

Reaching her final days, Mary kept the ring safely hidden in her room.

When she missed Frank, and wanted to feel close to him, she would often retrieve the ring and cradle it in her hand or slide it on her finger, reflecting on days long gone.

Finally, as Mary felt her time growing near, she passed the ring to her granddaughter, with the silent hope that her granddaughter might find a love so true as that of Mary and Frank.

While this story is purely fictional, as you can see, a ring such as this would be a virtual repository for imprinted life force. It all began when Frank chose the ring, and had the jeweler lay it aside. Each time Frank visited the local jeweler to make another payment, perhaps picking up the ring and dreaming of the day he might slide it on Mary's finger, he was unwittingly imprinting the ring by focusing his attention on both the ring and Mary. (Sending one stream of life force toward Mary, and another into the ring).

Mary, of course, imprinted the ring many times afterwards. Each time she held it, thought of Frank, and reflected on life, she imprinted the ring a bit more.

Now suppose that in present day, this ring somehow falls into the hands of a psychometrist or psychic. Because a psychometrist is sensitive to this resident life force energy, they can "read" the imprint(s) just like the blind might read Braille. When holding the ring, they pick up an image of a young coal-miner or blacksmith and his young fiancé. They might also discern the emotions Mary was feeling at the moment of each imprint. They might also see flashes and images from Mary's life – images of a husband leaving for war, of growing children, of Frank and Mary's home – the pictures in Mary's mind's eye that occurred during each imprint.

This, in basic terms, is how psychometry and imprinting works.

In the case of imprinting and psychometry, our hands allow us to make a direct connection with an object, and aid in reading any resident life force that remains in the item.

Along these same lines, an object that holds sentimental value for two (or more) persons can serve as a "bridge" or "conduit", connecting either a psychic (or ourselves) to "lost" loved ones.

Touch healing:

Touch healing interplays with this same "hands on" phenomenon.

As you may recall from grade school science lessons, when early scientists were studying sub-atomic particles and energy, they found that the outcome of their experiments were directly influenced by their expectations and thoughts.

Having said that, I'd like to present a question:

Have you noticed how – if you happen to bump your funny bone, accidentally cut yourself, or are otherwise injured – you instinctively grasp or hold the area near the injury?

If you have a headache, do you not touch your head?

If you're putting two and two together here, you now understand the basics of how touch healing works. By making a direct connection with an injury (or near the area) and sending a stream of "imprinting" life force into the area – and by expecting a certain outcome, on a sub-atomic level the cells begin to respond accordingly.

You may be wondering: "If this is the case, why don't cuts or bruises heal themselves when we first grab/touch them?"

The answer is blatantly simple: we expect a certain outcome. We don't expect the injury to "heal itself". Instead, we expect the injury to continue to exist and our touch to assuage the pain or discomfort.

And what happens?

Exactly what we expect.

As we'll discuss later, the activating element for successful touch-healing is belief.

"ESP" and Telepathy:

Have you ever been in a crowded room and sensed someone was staring at you?

Have you ever thought about someone – perhaps a relative in another state – only to have the phone ring and the caller be that specific person?

If you answered yes to either of these questions, there's a very simple explanation for how this phenomenon ties in with the exchange of life force.

As mentioned earlier, whenever we focus our attention toward another being or group, we send out a stream of life force toward that person or group. By this same token, whenever someone is sending life force to us, our subconscious mind detects the incoming stream and plays the role of a receptionist, or better yet: a "gatekeeper". This is to say, our subconscious mind tries to: (1) identify the source of the life force, (2) discern the intent of the sender, and (3) then notifies us (our conscious mind) so we have the choice of either raising or lowering our "guard".

This identification process works very similar to the way we "recognize" a person's voice. For example, if your mother calls you on the phone, she may begin speaking without identifying herself because she expects you to recognize her voice. And because there is a familiar pattern – certain tones and inflections – you will likely be able to recognize "mom" as the source of the call (and may immediately begin to determine the purpose [intent] of Mom's call).

In a parallel manner, your subconscious mind can recognize and identify the source of incoming life force streams by monitoring them for familiar patterns.

Let's take this one step further and look at an example many people can relate to:

Suppose your mother lives in another state, starts thinking about you, and decides to phone you to see how you are. By thinking about you, (focusing her attention on you), she unknowingly sends a stream of life force headed your way. Instantaneously, your subconscious perceives this incoming life force, recognizes the familiar pattern as belonging to "Mom", and then sends the cryptic message "Mom" to your conscious mind.

When the name Mom "inexplicably' pops into your mind, you find yourself wondering about her: how she is, and so on. About then, the phone usually rings and you find yourself telling your Mom: "Funny you called... I was just thinking about you".

This is a phenomenon I believe most people can relate with. We experience it, acknowledging in some way it is related to "ESP", yet (until now) we haven't understood how or why this phenomenon occurs.

By understanding the process, however, you can practice and begin to truly hone your ESP skills.

But let's go one step further...

In cases where your subconscious doesn't recognize the source of incoming energy, it may send a simple cryptic message such as "phone" or "doorbell".

In the case of someone staring at you in a crowded room, your subconscious has many options. It may send a message: "You're being admired by someone". It may choose to cause the hairs on the small of your neck to stand on end ("possible danger!"). Or it may provide a sensation of "eyes burning into the back of your head" ("someone's curious about you").

As mentioned, your subconscious first tries to identify the source of incoming life force. If it fails to find any familiar pattern within an inbound stream, it next tries to determine the intent of the sender based upon the overall polarity of the life force: positive, negative, or neutral.

Chapter 10
Positive, Negative, and Neutral Life Force

Whenever we send out life force, it carries a positive, negative, or neutral "polarity" – or a blend of any of these three, determined by our attitude toward the subject.

Put as simply as possible, whenever we focus our attention on a given subject, we infuse (imprint) our perception or opinion of the subject into the life force we are sending out.

This can be viewed as:

Good. Bad. Unbiased.

or

Positive. Negative. Neutral.

or (most accurately:)

Love. Fear. Indifference.

If you're beginning to sense a convergence about to take place – that is, two more universal gears meshing together – pat yourself on the back. As we learned earlier, our level of life force is interconnected with our emotional needs (and vise-versa). As the

85

level of our life force waxes and wanes, our emotional needs become unbalanced in order to restore balance to our life force. This symbiosis of "Life force level / Emotional Need" is:

a lesser cycle (that of life force exchange) operating within a grander cycle (that of our emotional needs).

We might liken this "lesser/grander cycle" relationship to the earth rotating upon its axis, bringing about the change between night and day. This change of night and day is a cycle in itself. Yet while it can stand alone, this same cycle is interconnected with many other cycles, both "lessor" and "grander". On the "grander" side, while the earth spins on its axis and brings about night and day, it also orbits the sun, bringing about the seasons. On the "lesser" side, the change between night and day interplays with cycles of animal behavior, plant growth, oceanic tides, and weather. And while all of these cycles are distinct and can be studied independently, they are each interconnected with the others and serve a purpose for the whole.

When our life force is low and we are depressed, our outlook in life becomes pessimistic. Because of this, we begin frequently sending out negative life force. That is, we have difficulty in finding "good" qualities in anything. We infuse negativity into most of our life force transmissions.

When our life force is high and our outlook is optimistic, we find "good" in everything and send out positive life force.

What's important to understand is this:

Whatever we send out eventually returns to us.

Good, bad, or indifferent – in this life or the next – whatever we "send out" eventually comes back. (Although not always in the exact same form, as will be demonstrated later).

If you're thinking ahead of the text here, you may already be putting two-and-two together. You see, the "gear of our life force" turns the "gear of our emotional needs", and the "gear of emotional needs" turns the "gear of our mood (emotions)". This gear then turns the "gear of our life circumstances", because what we send out, returns to us and manifests itself in our personal circumstances or environment.

If we continually send out positive life force, it grows and returns to us. (Hence the success of "positive thinking").

Likewise, when we send out negative life force, it also grows and returns to us.

If a person is depressed, and is sending out negative life force, they are inadvertently perpetuating their own cycle. By dwelling in pessimistic thoughts and behavior, they are casting land mines ahead on the very path they are following; land mines they will eventually have to detonate or carefully navigate.

Later, we'll discuss the "gear of our circumstances" in fuller detail. For now, however, we'll first explore the next gear in line, that of our "Mood" and "Emotions".

The Gear or Emotion/Mood:

In every life, there are triumphs and sorrows. There are moments of exuberance, and times of tribulation. There are days filled with bright sunny hope, and nights ruled by the darkest gloom.

At times we feel love or anger; generosity or greed, meekness or courage. At other times, we feel emotions such as hate, acceptance, or anguish. As humans, there is such a host of ranging emotions, it's often difficult to describe or define them in words.

What may shock you, however, is:

Only three pure emotions exist – love, fear, and indifference.

Everything else is a degree, or combination of these three base emotions.

Again we can use our color spectrum as an example. If one blends "blue" and "yellow", the result is a shade of green. Emotionally speaking, if one feels a combination of "fear" and "love", the result is reverence, awe, or respect – dependant upon the "shades" (degrees) of fear and love that are blended.

To better understand, let's look at the three primary emotions more closely.

FEAR (The negative):

Fear is the negative emotion. It is the emotion that cages and binds, and forces the erection of barriers.

Every road that is "paved with fear" is littered with potholes and unmarked curves. All the roads of fear lead to the same destination: one of hardship, heartbreak, and ultimate unhappiness.

Fear – not money – is the true root of all evil.

If you think about it, this becomes blatantly clear.

Money is an inanimate object. It can do both bad or good, dependant upon the hands that wield it and the hearts governing those hands. If fear rules the heart, and one fears they need money to survive (or be happy), this fear can drive one to enter a state-of-mind or attitude (mood) that encourages "sins" or "wrongdoing"; whatever it takes to get money and rid themselves of the fear.

In the highest sense, fear is the Bible's "Satan". This will become clearer and clearer as we progress.

As an example of fear (Satan) at work, we might consider the "sin" we call "pride". Pride unveiled is the fear of being inferior. If one fears being inferior, they are compelled to "prove to the world" (and themselves) that they are successful and therefore cannot be inferior. Thus, they brandish their accomplishments, assets, looks, prowess, or intelligence like a form of ID, proving (to themselves and others) they are not inferior. They do this seeking reassurance, based on their own fear of inferiority. Vanity, conceit, and egotism are each "shades" of color "pride"; as is narcissism, prejudice, and arrogance.

"Anger" is another feeling that is created by "the father of sin": fear. When we are hurt, we fear for our safety. As a method of self-protection, our pain becomes anger. Wrath, rage, revenge, irritation, and anguish are based on anger: the fear of being harmed or treated unjustly.

If you're particularly observant, you may note a connection here between fears such as pride, vanity, or anger, and the PM of "Intimidator".

"Doubt" is yet another hue upon the color wheel of fear. Doubt, worry, mistrust, hesitancy, and indecision are the fears of making poor decisions or taking inappropriate action. (Aloof and Interrogators)

"Coveting" is yet another example of a fear-induced state-of-mind. Coveting is the fear of being without (whatever is coveted). If one fears being without money, we call this fear "greed". If the "item" happens to be a person, we call this fear "jealousy". If the item is "the flesh", we call this fear lust. Avarice, cupidity, and selfishness are all shades of the color "covet": the fear of being without (Poor Mes).

But let's take this to the next level...

Fear begets certain states-of-mind, and these states-of-mind encourage certain behaviors.

For example, the "fear of being without" fathers coveting, and coveting can cause one to bury themselves in debt, to steal, to tell lies, or swindle and deceive in order to get whatever they covet (fear of being without).

As another example, the fear of being inferior sires pride, and pride can again persuade one to go into heavy debt, become a workaholic (to get things to show off), or to be fastidious and controlling.

Fear is the emotion that restricts and imprisons. It causes one to send out negative life force, and that negative life force grows and returns to us (often in different forms).

There are those who claim, however, that sins can be based on love (instead of fear). For example, in many Christian teachings, "lust" is often referred to as "the love of the flesh". On the surface, this teaching appears to be correct. However, upon higher thought and transcendence, we realize this line of thought is flawed.

"Lust" cannot exist within pure and perfect love, because the mere presence of lust desecrates the love and makes it impure, creating something corrupted that lies between love and fear.

For those of you who prefer more tactile or physical examples, suppose that you have two 5-gallon buckets. In one bucket, you have 2 gallons of pure water (love); in the other bucket, 2 gallons of toxic waste (fear). If you dip 1 gallon of the toxic waste and pour it into the water, what do you now have?

You now have two buckets of toxic waste: neither is pure, both are tainted.

Retrospectively, backing up and repeating the experiment from scratch, had you poured 1 gallon of the pure water into the toxic waste, the water itself would have remained pure. The toxic waste, however, would still be toxic waste, although it would be diluted.

Such a "dilution" is the state we equate to as ambivalence, when one feels a mixture of love and fear. Some of the stand-out emotions that pit our love against our fear are: jealousy, anguish, heartache, and grief.

What we learn through this edification is quite simple: while love can dilute and assuage fear, fear cannot exist within pure and unconditional love.

When you add toxic waste to pure water, the water becomes toxic waste.

If a fear such as "lust" exists in love, you have something other than pure love. Therefore, fear-based states-of-mind such as "lust" cannot be based in love, because the concept is flawed from its foundation.

There is no fear in love; but perfect love casteth out fear: because fear hath torment. He that feareth is not made perfect in love.
1 John 4: 18
The Bible
KJV

LOVE (The Positive):

Love is the emotion that allows freedom and breaks the bondage of fear. Regardless of the "shade" of love – be it appreciation, charity, admiration, fondness, delight, friendship, passion or tenderness – there can be no conditions or fear in pure love.

I believe John said this best in his first Epistle:

"And we have known and believed the love that God hath to us. God is love; and he that dwelleth in love dwelleth in God, and God in him."
Herein is our love made perfect, that we may have boldness in the day of judgment: because as he is, so are we in this world.
There is no fear in love; but perfect love casteth out fear: because fear hath torment. He that feareth is not made perfect in love.
1 John 4: 16-18
The Bible
KJV

Those of you who are particularly observant may have noticed that John did not capitalize "day of judgment". This would indicate that John was not referencing Biblical "Judgment Day", but was instead referring to a more generic type of "daily reckoning".

When combined with many of John's other teachings – such as "God is Love" and "he that dwelleth in love, dwelleth in God", it seems clear that John possessed a higher understanding of "love" and "fear" and the significance of "dwelling" in either. He clearly understood that "fear hath torment" while "love made perfect", and that dwelling in love would allow one "boldness" (the absence of fear) in not suffering torment or otherwise undesirable consequences.

Fortunately today, however, the expansiveness of the English language allows this lesson to be presented more definitively.

Whenever we think of a person or thing and have thoughts of appreciation, care, or concern, – thoughts based in love – we send out positive life force. The rewards we receive are therefore positive, favorable, and free of torment. In effect, they are benevolent and of God.

Positive life force – sincere appreciation – is the catalyst of creation, and the conduit that allows us to connect with God and all of creation.

NEUTRAL: Indifference:

Complete indifference is the "neutral" emotion and is one that is rarely "dwelled in" by humans, yet often governs members of the plant and animal kingdom. In a certain sense, the term "neutral" is a misnomer and is not completely whole or correct for our usage here. More aptly, we might substitute the term "Ground" for "Neutral", just as our electric circuits have leads for "hot", "common", and "ground".

Neutral or "grounded" emotion is the mere state of existence of an emotion (or energy) before it has been "polarized" with either fear or love (negative or positive, respectfully). It can also be an energy which has become "depolarized".

In effect, "neutral" or "ground" is the "inert" or "non-living": the catalyst of primary existence, the statement that "I am".

Depolarization:

Okay. You may be wondering by now, once energy has been polarized, how can it be "depolarized"?

93

There are many answers to this question because there are many types of energy that can be polarized. Using terms to ease comprehension, we might break these down into three primary groups: physical, emotional, and spiritual.

Physical Energies:

Any physical "non-living" object can be polarized through imprinting. If we look back to the story of "The Ring", we can see how Mary's ring – a form of energy – was the vehicle of both positive life force (love) and negative life force (worry).

Because of these resident polarizations, as long as this ring exists it will yield a certain "feel" to its owner. Eventually, the ring's "life" or existence will come to an end. This could occur through the ring being lost or discarded, or through it being sold and "melted down". Yet either way, whether the ring is recycled or undergoes a long, slow decomposition, the energy will eventually "cleanse itself". This is a bit more complicated than it sounds, but the details need not hamper us here.

Another form of imprinting (we might relate to) occurs when a physical dwelling becomes polarized. For example, if you go and walk through a used (empty) house, there is a completely different "feel" from that of walking through a new house that was just constructed. You can feel a residual presence of those who formerly lived there, even though they have vacated and left no possessions behind.

We often try to depolarize such a home and "make it our own" by giving it our own "touch". That is, we bring in items (new or used), we paint and remodel, to "mask" the polarization of the previous owners with that of our own.

As another example of depolarization of the "physical", any physical "body" also carries a host of positive and negative energies. These are formed through the host's experiences, through the perception of their body, and through any observer's perceptions. Once the body has "died" – that is, it is no longer inhabited by a soul – the body decomposes and these energies are restored to neutral.

Emotional and Spiritual:

As just mentioned, a host's body is polarized through their own perception of their body and character. Additionally, observers "add their two cents to this pot" whenever they "assess" or "judge" the body (or character) of another, thus imprinting that person with their opinion. As an end result, these varying charges of positive, negative, and neutral energy form what we commonly call one's "aura".

This aura is directly interlinked with self-perception, our life force level, our health, longevity, and the phenomenon we call "evolution".

Speaking in very general terms, "admirable people" – that is, persons who have a high ratio of favorable traits and pleasing physical features – are appreciated and therefore receive primarily positive imprints. Opposite to this, persons with a high ratio of negative traits – those whom society considers mentally or physically "inferior" – receive primarily negative imprints.

As an end result, the "inferior" are often saddled with a higher likelihood of suffering disease, hardship, and early death.

Why?

Because fear is like a "hot potato".

We instinctively want to get rid of it.

95

If we fear that we are in some way inferior, we eject our fear by throwing it on someone else. It's like children playing leapfrog. If someone jumps over us to prove they are "superior", we find someone "inferior" whom we can jump over to re-establish ourselves as one of the "superior".

A person who fears they are too short often silently snicker when a midget passes by.

The chubby man often laughs at the obese.

The "Smiths" strive to keep up with the "Jones'".

And so on.

As you probably know, our medical science has already made a correlation between fear and worries (aka: stress) and many of the diseases which plague humanity. In effect, we have learned we can "worry ourselves sick".

I tell you now this vein runs much deeper than it is commonly perceived or known. Being powerful, spiritual beings – a part of God – we not only have the innate ability to create and heal, we also have the ability to destroy and cause suffering – even if done so inadvertently.

As we will explore later, our words and thoughts are powerful tools. To protect us from ourselves, God gave us certain rules and installed certain Universal mechanisms that are designed to "balance the scales". One of the rules we've been told is: "judge not, lest ye be judged". Knowing what you now know, the purpose of this statement should have clearer and deeper meaning.

Directly correlated to this is the commandment:
"Thou shalt not bear false witness against thy neighbor".
(Exodus 20: 16, The Bible, KJV)

Again, if things are starting to fall together, a higher meaning for this commandment should be emerging. If a person "gossips" about their "neighbors", they imbue the neighbor with their negative (fear-based) opinion. What they fail to realize, however, is the "whole" of the neighbor's "aura" shapes their personal circumstances and environment. This, in turn, will eventually impact the gossiper.

Whatever you send out grows and returns to you; although not always in the exact same form.

Through love and appreciation, we acknowledge only the positive. By "judging", however, we acknowledge both the positive and the negative.

By judging and determining a certain trait, characteristic, or body feature is "inferior" or "bad", we harm the person we are judging through our negative thoughts. In effect, we raise the height of whatever hurdle they're already facing by weighing them down with our own fears.

Moreover, this same action is a double-edged sword. Not only does it add to the burden of the "inferior", it also creates our own fears (i.e."Boy, I'm sure glad I don't have that big, ugly tumor growing out of my cheek like that fellow! I wonder what causes that? I hope I never get it. Etc.").

Again, whatever you send out, grows and returns to you.

So what can you do if you accidentally judge, or do harm?

The answer is quite simple.

Since emotional and spiritual energies are intangible and never break down, they are depolarized in a very different manner than the physical; one which carries more significance for us. Depolarization occurs through what we call forgiveness and helping others – especially those who offend us.

How is that?

We "cancel out" a negative with an equal or greater positive.

The process begins by first recognizing a fear, and then appreciating it for what it is.

To aide in edification, let's assign some mock values to "fears" and "appreciations" so we might use math as a virtual "gauge" for the intangibles of fear and appreciation.

For our purposes here, let's assume that the "fear of being overweight" holds a value of "-10". This fear is "negative" in its absolute value because fears are negative and undesirable.

Let's also assume that appreciating the "fear of being overweight" holds a value of "10". And since appreciation is a positive, the absolute value of this appreciation would be "+10".

Taking this one step further, let's also assume that one receives "5 bonus points" for recognizing a fear (such as the fear of being overweight), because one must first "recognize" (realize a fear exists) before they can appreciate it. What I'm saying here is, one can possess a fear of being overweight without realizing they have that fear; but in order to appreciate the fear, they must first recognize their fear and realize it exists.

With this "recognition bonus", appreciation now holds a value of "15" (10 + 5).

Having established these mock values, let's assume there are two co-workers: "A" and "B". We'll say that worker "A" possesses a fear of being overweight, while "B" does not. The score at this point would be:

"A"	"B"
-10	0

Let's also assume that during a heated disagreement at work, worker "A" (fearing he/she might be overweight) makes a snide remark about co-worker "B" being overweight.

By doing this, "A's" intention is to throw their "hot potato of fear" upon worker "B". Mistakenly, "A" feels that if he/she can point out someone else is "fatter" than themselves, he/she will no longer be subject to their fear. They justify this to themselves by thinking: "Since I'm not as fat as this person, I have less to worry about (fear)".

Using math as a standard here, you can see how this does not work. Regardless of whether or not "B" believes "A's" comment and adopts the fear, "A" still possesses their fear.

A's score is still:

"A"
-10.

"A" can spend their entire life poking fun at "fat people" and making "fat jokes", but they will continually gain no lasting satisfaction from their comments. To the contrary, they will only deepen their own fear through seeing how others are affected by their comments. Their only chance to ever truly escape their fear is to realize it is a fear, and appreciate the fear for what it is.

As for worker "B", if some part of "B" believes "A's" comment, the score goes to:

"A"	"B"
-10	-10

As you can see here, "A" has not passed off their "hot potato of fear". Instead, they have only infected another person, thus spreading their own fear to "B".

When this occurs, if "A" sees that their comment affected "B", "A" mistakenly feels "they won" and feel "they elevated themselves to a level equal to or greater-than "B". What they fail to realize, however, is they have not gone up at all, they have only succeeded in bringing "B" down.

There are no winners in this scenario: only two losers.

But let's change that result through a different response from "B".

Let's return to the initial scores ("A" = -10; "B" = 0) and assume that after "A" hurls their "spear-of-fear insult", "B" recognizes "A's" fear of being overweight, and appreciates the fear for what it is.

The score is now:

"A"	"B"
-10	+15

In effect, it appears that "B" has "won", and in a sense "B" has. Yet the ultimate "win" occurs if "B" can help "A" recognize and dissolve their fear.

The risk of ending or dropping the conflict here is, while "B" escaped the infection of "A's" fear, "A" still possesses the fear and will continue to infect others in a futile and non-ending attempt to rid themselves of their fear. "A" may infect "C", "D", "E", "F" (and so on), and because of so many people eventually sharing "A's" fear, "B" may begin to doubt their initial judgment ("this fear must be worse than I thought because so many people are worried about it..."). Thus, creating circumstances that later causes "B" to step in the mud-puddle they just side-stepped.

To truly "win", "B" must go one step further and attempt to dissolve "A's" fear. As mentioned, this occurs through forgiveness and helping others. It must not be driven by "pride" with an "I'm better than him/her and must stoop and help them" attitude. Nor can it be driven by any other fear.

Instead, it must be driven by sincere concern or love.

Blessed are the pure in heart: for they shall see God."
Matthew 5: 8
The Bible
KJV

By forgiving "A" of his comment (in a very sincere manner – pure of heart), "B" loosens the grip of fear holding "A". What "A" sees is that his comment didn't have the intended impact, and therefore the issue may not be as significant as he feared.

"...Forgive, and ye shall be forgiven."
Luke 6:37
The Bible
KJV

Secondly, if "B" is able to help "A" realize – recognize – his fear, and appreciate it for what it is, "A" will be freed of his fear.

The score:

"A"	"B"
5	15

Two winners; no losers.

I tell you now, however, this is not an easy task because many people do not want to forfeit their fears.

Fear is the only tool they know.

As a race, we thrive upon fear. We demand it in the latest blockbuster, the current bestseller, in our news, in roller-coasters and rides, in sports events, and even in game shows. When a world event occurs, such as the destruction of the World Trade centers, we find ourselves glued to the media, savoring fear, awaiting the next turn of events.

Why?

The answer here is simple. Just as "A" mistakenly feels he/she can lessen their fear of being overweight by pointing out "they are not as overweight as 'B'", we try to escape our own fears through focusing on "worse" fears experienced by others. Our misplaced goal is to make our own fears "less" by acknowledging "more".

We call this "escapism". However, as we all too well know, escapism is temporary "escape" at best. Sooner or later, after the sensational has faded, our "minor" fears return in full effect.

What we must strive to realize is, rather than attempting to downplay our own fears by comparing them to "worse", we can free ourselves from fear's grip through recognizing each fear and appreciating it for what it is.

As ironic as it is, some people fear giving up their fears. In the truest sense, they worship "Satan" or live on "The Dark Side of The Force".

Returning to our example of "A" and "B", what "B" might attempt when "A" throws his "spear of fear", is first defusing the situation. That is, pausing, smiling (sincerely), patting "A" on the shoulder (or offering a handshake), and saying something such as: "We've known each other a long time... I know you didn't mean that, Buddy. And if you did, maybe you're right... Why don't we sleep on this and talk about it tomorrow over lunch?"

At lunch the following day, "B" might start things off by explaining how his aunt weighed 300 pounds, but lived to be 100.

"B" may not be able to "win" this battle in one fell swoop. "B" may not be able to win at all. But even if "B" "fails", "B" can walk away from the experience knowing they tried, and perhaps with the opportunity to learn something from an otherwise unfortunate incident.

The question I ask you is, if we learn from any experience – be the event pleasant or unpleasant – do we really ever "fail"?

"But I say unto you, That ye resist not evil: but whosoever shall smite thee on thy right cheek, turn to him the other also.
And if any man will sue thee at the law, and take away thy coat, let him have thy cloke also.
And whosoever shall compel thee to go a mile, go with him twain [two]"
Matthew 5: 39-41
The Bible
KJV

How can one be sincere or sympathetic in a situation like "B's"?

There are three simple steps:

1. We must first realize that fear exists.

    While we are each independently-thinking spiritual beings, and are each a part of God, we each face the challenge of surviving in a "human" environment, replete with "human" conditions, perceptions, and fallacies. Due to this, we all have times of "temptation" which cause us to fall prey of fear (aka: Satan...evil...bad...wrongdoing – fear has a "legion" of names).

103

2. Secondly, after we realize "fear exists", we can begin the forgiveness process by recognizing that we have "fallen" at times, and the "offender" can also fall prey to fear. Whatever "wrong" they have perpetrated is based on fears of their own. When calling someone a name such as "fat", the offender possesses the actual fear of being "fat"; otherwise their remark would have no value. For example, if they called you a name they didn't fear but instead admired (positive), the result would be a compliment or endearment rather than an insult.

    Whether this perpetrator stole from you, betrayed your trust, cheated, misled you, or perpetrated any of a myriad of other "wrongs", their action was driven by their own fears.

3. After we have recognized that fear exists, and we each fall prey to it, this provides "common ground" that allows us to relate to and sympathize with the offender. Forgiveness comes naturally, and comfort is provided through understanding.

Blessed are the merciful: for they shall obtain mercy.
Matthew 5: 7
The Bible
KJV

Again: love releases, fear enslaves.

OUR GOAL:

To live abundantly, the goal we strive to reach is one of always sending out positive life force. If you re-read the New Testament with this principle in mind, you will see that Christ tried to teach this lesson through example. During the day He walked the Earth, "science" had not yet been born. The concept of "energy" was beyond the comprehension of humankind at that time. Thus, Christ tried to teach through living example, showing ways to elucidate the positive and appreciate the simplicities of life.

We can improve our own lives right now.

You are currently on the path to learning how to do this, but our journey is not complete.

Journey on. Seek, and ye shall find.

A Quick Recap

Are you beginning to grasp the concept of all things being energy?

If you are, you're a very quick learner! Good for you!

If not – don't worry – it takes time. When I've explained this in person to someone, the other person often can't get a handle on it right away. What inevitably happens is they show up two or three days later, their face beaming, and I know they've grasped it before they can blurt it out. I know they've seen things through the course of day-to-day life, and several puzzle pieces have suddenly snapped together. So if you haven't got it yet, don't worry.

Said most aptly: "Fear not".

The next two sections will help you even more by showing examples you can see in everyday life. You WILL learn to multiply. Don't lose sight of that and don't give up.

Before we move on, let's take a moment to recap, summarize, and add some brief points to what we've learned:

1. Energy is the base element of ALL matter; ALL things are energy. God made ALL things and God is ALL things. Therefore, we are each God and God is us.

105

2. We all have certain needs and these needs help us maintain a healthy emotional balance.

Moreover, these needs play a bigger part of the picture. They are a cycle of evolution.

They are how we grow as a "being". Today, we are focusing on our spiritual needs.

Next week, we may focus on our family needs. Next month, we may have a subconscious theme of improving our social needs. Next year, our subconscious goal may be to improve our romantic needs.

As we focus and learn about each need, we grow as a being, and the cycle continues.

3. We all have a Life force and our moods and needs are driven by our energy level at the time. When our life force is high, we feel great. We think clearly and we're ready to go out and work off or share some of this energy with the rest of the world! When our Life force is low, we feel down and need time to rejuvenate. We often do this by being alone, spending time with family (our sanctuary), or communing with God as we seek hope and guidance.

This life force is the part of God He used to create us. It exists in ALL living things. And it is shared by all things.

Unwittingly, we compete for it. We desire it. We block it from being stolen, and steal it from others.

Part Two

Chapter 11
Building Faith

By now you may be wondering how such tasks as learning to identify personality modes, learning about our emotional needs, and learning about life force polarities could possibly relate to the getting "anything you want", right?

In order to "get anything you want", you will need to have unfaltering faith in the energy principle and how it interacts with the universe. And in order to have this level of faith, you must truly believe. You must believe this just as you believe in the existence of air. Although you can't see it or touch it, you know that air is there, sustaining your life.

Now that you know about the four different PM's, as you go about your daily life, you will begin to identify them in people you know. You will see this phenomenon at work. More importantly, you will begin to see how people use their PM's to rob energy from others. You will also catch yourself doing it. And as you become aware of what's happening, and see it occurring over and over, you will begin to believe. Once that belief saturates you, faith will follow naturally.

Before we move on to the next lesson, we'll take a look at one other brief example of the energy transference that grounds us and connects us to God: the All and Everything.

If you're beginning to grasp the concept of all things being energy, the next time you eat an apple or orange (or slab of steak), you'll look at it differently. At a sub-atomic level, you're ingesting energy. The proteins and chemicals clinging to that energy make the apple taste differently from the orange, but at a sub-atomic level, it is still energy. Our body sorts out this energy, and deposits the "waste products" back to the earth. And in those waste products are fragments of our own energy.

We also "sweat" and fragments of our energy evaporate from the skin, are purified in the process, and return to the universe. In time, those same fragments may return to us, or, more likely, they become part of something else.

We know that energy is eternal. It may change forms, such as water turning to steam or sunlight turning to heat as it passes through a pane of glass; nonetheless, it is still energy and it will continue to exist.

All energy in current existence came from God. And because we know energy is eternal, ALL things ARE God. They always have been; always will be.

"A human being is part of the whole called by us universe, a part limited in time and space. We experience ourselves, our thoughts and feelings as something separate from the rest. A kind of optical delusion of consciousness. This delusion is a kind of prison for us, restricting us to our personal desires and to affection for a few persons nearest to us. Our task must be to free ourselves from the prison by widening our circle of compassion to embrace all living creatures and the whole of nature in its beauty...We shall require a substantially new manner of thinking if mankind is to survive."[6]

Albert Einstein

Chapter 12

Transcending the Four Primary Personality Modes

There are two remaining personality modes which I haven't yet discussed, and they are the first steps of spiritual transcendence. These are called: "The Life of the Party" and "Spiritual" mode.

As spiritual beings and part of God, it is our mission to evolve and grow. And as we ascend the ladder of growth, these two Personality Modes are the "higher rungs" we inherently strive to reach – often without realizing they are our ultimate objectives.

THE "LIFE OF THE PARTY"

In rare crossings of life, we sometimes encounter a person whose mere presence seems to "brighten the room". These luminaries are often described or endeared as "bubbly", "full of life", and "eternally optimistic", yet there's something special about them that we can't quite put a finger on. They are surrounded by excitement and are often termed "the life of the party". People are drawn to them like sharks at a feeding frenzy.

Now that you have a handle on the exchange of life force, you can probably see how this evolution occurs. When a person steps outside the circle of the four primary PM's and begin to freely share their life force, their own life force grows. The more they share, the more they grow, and therefore they can maintain their openness without erecting the shields of the four primary PM's.

This personality mode is closely related to our emotional need for "social time". It is why we crave time celebrating with our peers. At a subconscious level, we know that through such celebration, we can gather life force. But up until now, you may not have understood why: the motor was hidden beneath the hood.

The one flaw with this Personality Mode is the source. Because of personal economics, most people can't afford to live at parties or always have an event going on. The source is inconsistent... and there is a better way. Another rung up the ladder.

THE "SPIRITUAL" MODE

The Spiritual mode is the highest visible rung upon our PM ladder. Through this mode, we connect to the eternal source of life force: that of God.

By "paying attention" and appreciating every part of nature we encounter – plants, animals, weather, humans, etc., – and by paying reverence to God – we are connected to God and "All of Him" (the universe) and can thereby draw all the POSITIVE energy we need.

We never need an outside source.

When Jesus walked the Earth, he knew this. His words conveyed and repeated this message. This is the spiritual basis for "fasting in the wilderness".

Our Monks and Spiritual "gurus" also know this. We portray them in our movies as living in monasteries amid lavish gardens, yet we fail to comprehend "why" their days are spent tediously pruning the shrubbery. We sense an almost palpable serenity in their environment, yet we fail to "connect the dots".

By communing with Nature and God, we can connect to the eternal source of energy any time we need our own life force recharged. And by doing so, we recharge the life force of others (plants/nature). We give, and we receive.

Chapter 13
Thoughts and Beliefs

Matter is energy.
Thoughts are tools.
Belief is the driving force.

THOUGHTS

As we've already discussed: "all matter is energy".

"Thoughts" are also energy, and can be used to influence matter: to create. In order to create, we'll need to start thinking of them in that context.

Be forewarned, however, that later we'll be looking at a "curve ball" in the creation process. I'll explain, when the time arrives.

Returning to "thoughts", the good news now is you probably already perceive "thoughts" as forms of energy. This is because thoughts hold the characteristics we naturally attribute to energy. That is, they are non-tangible and behave like energy.

In an article titled The Mystery of Matter and Energy[7], published by Twelve Star Publishing, author Guy McCarthy stated:

"In other words, if you break matter and energy down into the smallest possible portions, there is nothing physical left. All you have is a set of mathematical equations. This means that the finest structure of the universe is merely information. But what is information? It is an idea. And what is an idea? It is the basic unit of consciousness. ... Matter and Energy are made from the same, non-physical stuff. And the stuff is called consciousness."

Well said, Guy.

Unless you have very sophisticated medical equipment on hand, it's impossible to "see" thoughts. And even with the right equipment, if you try to look inside a human brain and actually "see" thoughts, all you see are "sparks" (small bursts of energy) jumping from one neurotransmitter to another.

We can hear our own thoughts (and sometimes the thoughts of others), but we can not taste them or touch them or smell them. And all of this makes it easy to accept that thoughts are a form of energy.

What are thoughts besides energy?

According to my trustworthy, dog-eared desk copy of The Merriam-Webster Dictionary, the word "thought" is defined as follows:

"Thought: The process of thinking; a serious consideration; contemplation; regard; the power to imagine; reasoning; opinion; notion; idea; concept."

As you can see, Merriam-Webster has provided a clean, working definition. But let's take it one step further...

Thoughts are "clumps of words" formed together.

And like thoughts, "words" are energy. We can see them in text, but they cannot be touched, smelled, or tasted. We can print them out, but what we have as a finished product is ink on paper, arranged in the shape of words – shapes we (humankind) have

116

assigned to alphabet letters, in order to form words. We can "hear" the sound we use for a word, and we can think words, but we can't physically grasp an actual word. Words are intangible because words are energy.

Words, in themselves, are identifiers. Whether they are nouns, participles, verbs, adjectives, or any other part of grammar, they each have a specific meaning and use. When used correctly, they help us assemble and convey our thoughts.

For example, the simple word "hungry" conveys the concept of "feeling hunger", but it's not a complete "thought" until we string it together with other words. When chained together with other words, such as "I am (hungry)" or "you are (hungry)" or "the goldfish is (hungry)", we have a precise and complete thought that we can convey to others.

In a strong sense, words are our "tools". We use them to build thoughts, and with thoughts, we can build much more.

To comprehend the true power of words, we need only read the first chapter of Genesis. When God said "Let there be light", there was light. And whenever He spoke, His will was accomplished through words.

Like words, thoughts are powerful. They are even more powerful than words.

Why?

Think of "words" as the ammunition for a gun. A word in itself can do no harm. Your thoughts, however, already contain words. They are like playing with a loaded gun. Do you not think using words? Therefore, whatever we think can potentially be manifested. The full process is only missing one ingredient – belief – which pulls the trigger.

117

BELIEF

Our thoughts are driven by emotion.

When we listen to someone speak, we can often hear the emotion in their voice. "Belief" is a form of emotion. When we speak about something we believe in, we speak with "conviction". Yet belief differs from emotions because: not only is it an emotion, it is also a state of mind.

If you think of most of the emotions we feel – joy, anger, fear, love, hate, anguish, sadness, happiness, etc. – you will realize that they occur naturally within us.

A "belief", however, was born to us as a thought or concept. It's a thought that we know is true because we've pondered and reviewed it. We've mulled it over and over, weighed the pros and cons; and in our heart it feels true. Our intuition that God uses to guide us has "stamped its approval". And once that occurs and God tells us "This is true", we become very passionate about our new belief.

It then becomes the new platform upon which we weigh and test other potential beliefs.

Belief is the driving force of thoughts.

And what are thoughts?

Tools, right?

Are things starting to click into place?

Therefore I say unto you, What things soever ye desire, when ye pray, believe that ye receive [them], and ye shall have [them].

Mark 11:24
The Bible
KJV

Chapter 14
The Divinity Formula

Matter is clumps of energy – the material we use for building.
Thoughts are clumps of words – the tools we use to build.
Belief is a driving force – it controls and actuates the tools.

The Third Law of the Universe is this:

Whatever we believe we are: we are.

It's that simple.

If you think you are fat – and you believe it with unfaltering faith – you will be fat.
If you think you are poor – and you believe it – you will be poor.
If you think that you are wealthy – and you believe it – you will be wealthy.
If you think that you can heal – and you believe it – you will be able to heal.

And the list goes on...

This is intrinsically linked with our fears and loves, and how those fears and loves shape our personal circumstances, our environment, and our lives. Yet it extends even beyond these realms, as we'll later discuss.

Now that you have a general understanding of matter, thoughts, and belief, let's break down the process and look at how it works. I will take this chance, however, to encourage you to read the rest of this book. The information covered later, after you have the formula for "getting what you want", is critical for achieving happiness.

Remember our lesson about "multiplication"?

Assuming you do, consider the later chapters of this book as "division" and "algebra". The "division" will allow you to check your multiplication – a skill you'll need if things aren't working. The "algebra" will deepen your understanding of math overall, including working with "negative figures".

So let's get started...

In the movie Terminator 2, Judgment Day[8], there is a scene in which the "villain" terminator was frozen by liquid nitrogen and shattered into millions of little pieces. For those of you who saw the movie, you may remember this scene... because just when you thought the T-1000 was finally dead, and all was well, those little bits and pieces of his body began to thaw and started flowing back together, like liquid mercury to a magnet, reforming him.

I point this out because this concept roughly equates to how matter is formed or manipulated. On a level we can't see, our thoughts gather bits of energy. Like-type-thoughts attract other like-type-thoughts and collectively guide this energy into a specific shape. The driving factor – the actuator of the process – is belief. And through repetition, matter is formed.

Like the radio waves that bounce all around you, like the electricity flowing silently and invisibly through wires and cords, you need not see this phenomenon to know it exists. The "materials" are already present – they've been there all along. The tools – your thoughts – are also present and have been there all along. As a matter of fact, they've been continuously working for you all your life. All you've needed to have "anything you want" is understanding and belief.

It's that simple.

> Jesus said unto him, If thou canst believe, all things [are] possible to him that believeth.
> Mark 9:23
> The Bible
> KJV

> And Stephen, full of faith and power, did great wonders and miracles among the people.
> Act 6:8
> The Bible
> KJV

We've been given this message time-and-time again, yet we have failed to comprehend it's simplicity. Everything you need to perform a "miracle" is already present. You've simply needed the knowledge, and belief.

Divinity through belief:

If you sit quietly, close your eyes and "visualize" a $50.00 bill lying on the surface in front of you – and believe without doubt that a $50.00 bill is there – through practice you will be able to produce a genuine $50.00.

You need not memorize the exact details of a $50.00 bill for your visualization. The details will care for themselves. The key to success is believing a $50.00 bill is in front of you. You do not need to mentally "construct" the bill, the visualization is merely intended to strengthen your own belief.

Seeing is believing.

You must believe this will occur – has occurred – with the same belief that if you inhale, oxygen will flood your lungs. You must believe with intractable conviction and faith that, when you open your eyes – before you have opened your eyes – a $50.00 bill is already in front of you. And when you can do this, you will have your $50.00 bill. This method of matter-production works, but it requires unwavering faith and lots of practice.

As an aid, we can further strengthen the efficacy of the divinity process by infusing words into the process. If, while visualizing our $50.00 bill, you vocalize your belief (i.e.: "There is a $50.00 bill on the table in front of me... etc., etc.") we add to the process. Moreover, if there is conviction in your voice as you say the words, you supplement the process even more.

It all comes down to belief.

In the Bible, Christ tried to teach this through many lessons. In one such example, appearing in St. Mark 17, a man presented his boy (a "lunatic" as he called him) for Jesus to heal, and Jesus cast out the "demon" (a mental illness), curing the boy "from that hour". The apostles who witnessed the miracle then asked Jesus why they (being apostles of Christ) were unable to perform such a feat.

And Jesus said unto them: "Because of your unbelief: for verily I say unto you, If ye have faith as a grain of mustard seed, ye shall say unto this mountain, Remove hence to yonder place; and it shall remove; and nothing shall be impossible to you.
St. Matthew 17:20
The Bible
KJV

124

As we'll look at later, Christ had to teach and re-teach this lesson many times before his followers "got it". As strange as it may seem, we have been using our Divinity unknowingly throughout all of our lives, without giving it a second thought. Yet when we try to purposely use it, we fail. This "failure" occurs because of our acquired thinking. It's similar to the infant who is placed in a swimming pool, and immediately begins to swim. Yet later in life, when that same infant has grown into a man, he drowns when falling overboard from his fishing boat because he believes he doesn't know how to swim.

The good news is, this is the hard way to use the formula for "getting what you want".

There is a much easier way, with the help of God.

I only point out the previous visualization technique because it's one of the best methods for self-healing what traditional medicine can't treat. We see evidence of this in our medical facilities that treat "the whole person" (instead of just the disease), addressing the whole person's emotional, spiritual, and physical needs.

Knowing what you now know, understanding how our life force energy level controls our emotional and spiritual needs, and how these needs moderate our outlook, and how our outlook (what we send out) shapes our personal circumstances, you should now have a handle on why "whole person" treatments can succeed where traditional medicine fails. This is especially true when combined with positive affirmations (such as telling yourself "I am healthy") and visualizing a tumor receding, being eaten by white blood cells, or vanishing altogether.

Patients at "whole person" facilities receive lots of positive attention. Thus, their life force is balanced. And often inadvertently, they learn to tap their own divinity without comprehending the underlying mechanics or even realizing the process has occurred.

Hopefully, another puzzle piece just clicked into place. But if not, read on...

Tapping God's Divine "Delivery Service":

For the easiest way of attaining your desires, all you have to do is thank God for what you already have – and believe that you have it.

I call this mode of creation: "Delivery Service".

Why?

Because whatever you thank God for, and believe you have, is delivered right into your life.

As stated in Neale Donald Walsch's Conversations with God, An Uncommon Dialogue, Book 1[9], the author attributes God as saying:

"The correct prayer is therefore never a prayer of supplication, but a prayer of gratitude.
When you thank God in advance for that which you choose to experience in your reality, you, in effect, acknowledge it is there... in effect. Thankfulness is thus the most powerful statement to God; an affirmation that even before you ask, I have answered."

Here again, the key is faith. It is believing with intractable faith that everything you want and need is already provided. When you can believe this, you will have everything you want and need.

Before I provide simple step-by-step instructions for actuating the "Delivery Service" method of divinity, I need to clarify a couple of points. You will notice in certain upcoming statements that I refer to "The Universe" instead of referring to "God". It's important here that I clarify why I will do such. There are two primary reasons; the first being one of distinction. By ascribing a name to "God", the mere assignment of such implies that God is a separate being from ourselves. That He is completely independent from everything you know to exist, and such thinking defies and denies our own Divinity. We are created not only by God, but also of God. "God" is all things. And in that equation – we, being "some thing", being a part of this All and Everything, are each a part of God.

In effect, by being a part of God, we collectively are God – the Universe.

As an example, we might look at the human body. The human body is a single functioning unit in itself. Yet at the same time, each body is made up various "parts". We have bones and organs, blood and muscle, tendons, nails, skin, hair, glands, and a host of other "parts" that all work in unison as the whole.

Dissecting that one step further, each one of these "parts" is made up of billions and billions of "individuals" we refer to as "cells". We have brain cells to form the brain, nerve cells to form nerve, muscle cells for muscle and tooth cells for teeth.

In effect, these "groups" of cells parallel "life as we know it". Life in our physical world – Earth – is made up by thousands of different species. There are cattle, dogs, humans, cats, monkeys, zebra, tigers, frogs, fish, snakes, birds, trees and bees (and more species than we need to list here). And while each group of these species is made up by thousands or billions of "individuals", they are each a "part of the whole".

It all begins with energy, and ultimately returns to energy. Rather than just "dust to dust; ashes to ashes", our reality is "energy to energy".

Returning to our subject, the second reason I choose to use the term "Universe" is one of psychological basis. As humans, many of us are reluctant to "ask" anyone – even God – for anything. The mere act of "asking" implies that we are weak and helpless. It implies that we are unable to control our own lives and circumstances – much less our own destiny. In effect, by "asking", we are denying our divinity. This creates "doubts and fears" in our mind, undermining the wall of faith we need to succeed.

The "Delivery Service" is not actuated through "begging" (Poor Me), nor is it driven through "demanding" what we want (as the Intimidator might), nor through questioning how the process works (Interrogator), nor ignoring the process completely (Aloof). It is activated through love and appreciation – by considering ourselves as part of the whole – the "Universe" – and by knowing that every need we have will be fulfilled through God's love.

"Behold the fowls of the air: for they sow not, neither do they reap, nor gather [food] into barns; yet your heavenly Father feedeth them. Are ye not much better than they?"
St. Matthew 6:26
The Bible
KJV

"...Consider the lilies of the field, how they grow; they toil not, neither do they spin: And yet I say unto you, That even Solomon in all his glory was not arrayed like one of these."
St. Matthew 6:28,29
The Bible
KJV

To actuate the Delivery Service, we need only love and appreciate all those with whom we come in contact. This applies to every plant, animal, or person – every "cell" and part of the "Universe".

By doing this, by finding the "good" in all, we in effect are "praising God". And through that relationship, all of our wants and needs are fulfilled.

> But I say unto you, Love your enemies, bless them that curse you, do good to them that hate you, and pray for them which despitefully use you and persecute you.
> Matthew 5:44
> The Bible
> KJV

Step 1 – Creating a place to commune with God:

If you have a present relationship with God, you may already have a certain place and time of day that you "commune" with Him. Perhaps you pray each night before going to bed, or during quiet afternoons when you have the house to yourself, or perhaps even during respites in the bathroom.

If you don't have a relationship with God, a good way to prepare for this relationship is by setting aside a "special place". While you can talk to God anytime (and anywhere) by merely focusing your attention toward Him, it's often comforting to have a sacred retreat where you can meet with God: a space free of interruptions and worries, that allows you to enter a spiritual mood.

You'll want a place where you can sit or lie in comfort, and can burn candles if they help you feel more spiritually attuned.

I should mention here that candles are not at all necessary for success in using "the delivery service"; rather, they help to enhance a spiritual ambiance, and are also comforting and calming in nature, aiding in forgetting fears and embracing love.

Because you are communing with God, if you should opt to use candles, the colors white, purple, or gold are the most appropriate. Respectively speaking, these colors represent pureness, spirit, and riches.

Secondly, I would recommend always using candles in groups of "3". This is because 3 is the divine number (as we'll discuss later).

For many people, the bedroom is the most suitable space for your communion with God. If you're fortunate enough to have an unused room you can commandeer, that much the better. For reasons we'll discuss later, I would recommend that this special place have electricity and a radio. If that isn't possible, a portable radio will do.

As one other mention, whenever you prepare to commune with God, be sure to disconnect/disable your phone or beeper to help avoid interruption.

Step 2 – Other preparations:

Once you have a place prepared where you meet with God, before you begin communing, take a walk in the woods or a local park if that's possible.

Why?

It's a two-fold reason.

First, taking such a walk will revitalize you with positive Life force – the catalyst of creation.

Second, anytime we're around nature it's easy to feel connected to the Universe and God. When we see the splendor of birds and plants, the majesty of clouds in the skies and the sun shimmering off surfaces, the whole experience can be ethereal, yet grounding. Instead of being surrounded by cold manmade products (i.e. metal-framed chairs, laminated wood surfaces, plastic, drywall, etc.), taking a walk merges us with the warmth of true creation. It reminds us that we are part of the larger scene, not merely a visitor or spectator.

Were it not for the swings of weather (and allergies), a spot in the woods might be the most effective place to commune with our Creator. However, with time being in such short supply, you'll want to have access to the place you have set aside for God day or night, rain or shine. Later, after you've tapped "The Delivery System", you'll have more free time to work with.

Step 3 – The opening prayer:

After you've taken that walk, return to your place of communion, and light any candles you may have prepared. Sit, or lie, and allow your body to relax.

Say the following prayer.

Why?

Because it in itself is an affirmation of the highest sense.

Our father which are all things,
Praise to you,
I thank you for your guidance as I pass through life's journey;
I thank you for allowing me to be whatever I wish; to experience all I can be; to create, as we have done together, before.
I thank you for supplying my daily food, and all those things

131

which allow me to live this life to the fullest.
I thank you for loving me; as I love all those I encounter.
I thank you for giving me good health; and for watching over my home and family.
I thank you for the beauty and splendor I find in nature.
I thank you for all that you are; all that I am, and all that can be.
Amen

As an alternative to the above prayer, you can also recite the prayer of David, which is an affirmation in itself (as demonstrated by the comments in parenthesis):

The Lord is my shepherd, I shall not want.
He maketh me to lie down in green pastures
(He provides me rest).
He leadeth me beside the still waters.
(I shall not thirst).
He restoreth my soul.
(I shall not need life force).
He leadeth me in the paths of righteousness for his name's sake.
(I shall be guided by Him).
Yea, thou I walk through the valley of the shadow of death, I will fear no evil.
(I shall not fear).
For thou art with me.
(I shall not be lonely or without God).
Thy rod and thy staff comfort me.
(I shall not need comfort).
Thou preparest a table before me in the presence of mine enemies.
(I shall not hunger, nor be hated).
Thou anointest my head with oil; my cup runneth over.
(I shall live in abundance).
Surely goodness and mercy shall follow me all the days of my life.

(I shall live happily).
And I will dwell in the house of the Lord for ever.
(I shall live with God, forever).

Psalm 23,
The Bible
KJV

Step 4 – Affirmations:

After you have prayed, continue to sit or lie down (whichever is most comfortable) and merely allow yourself to relax. The key here is, after getting that adrenaline flowing from the walk, as you "come down" your mind will quickly enter into alpha mode[10]. Alpha mode is a state where we are very relaxed, yet still conscious. It's the state we enter just before falling asleep at bedtime. As the conscious mind becomes sluggish, the subconscious begins "waking up" and preparing to take over.

As you relax, you'll need to prepare a "positive affirmation". Your positive affirmation will be a short phrase thanking God for whatever it is you "want" added to your life. The key here is to never include the words "ask", "want", or "will" in your script.

Why?

It's very simple. God (the Universe) will manifest exactly – and I can't express this strongly enough here – exactly – whatever you tell it to manifest. In other words, if you decide that money is what you need to be happy, and you tell God: "I want money", that exact statement will manifest itself: You will want money. Through natural occurrences in our lives, God – the Universe – will manifest exactly what we state. So if you tell the Universe "I want money", within a week you may find that you lose your job, or the car engine breaks down and needs replacing, or some type of unexpected calamity befalls your life so "you want money" and your "request" has been fulfilled.

As you can see, this coincides with our earlier lessons on "fear". If you fear being "poor", and you fear you "can't be happy without money", you are casting landmines ahead of yourself on the very path you are following. By (unwittingly) thinking and believing that "you are poor" or "you are unhappy without money", you inadvertently manifest these circumstances through them being your "affirmations".

At first glance, this might seem a bit cruel on God's behalf. However, it's important to understand that God does not judge what we ask for and decide on a case-by-case basis whether or not we deserve it − "good" or "bad". Instead, God merely provides whatever we request. Through us, He experiences All − both good and bad − and He will enable us to experience either extreme without prejudice by merely fulfilling whatever we request.

The request is completely up to you − "good" or "bad" − chosen through our own free will.

As another example of making a request in the wrong manner, if you choose an affirmation such as: "I will receive money", you will never actually receive the money.

Why?

Because you are telling the Universe you will − at some unknown point in the future − receive money. Therefore, you don't have it now.

Understanding the relevance of this can get a little tricky, so allow me to try to loosely explain.

In our perception of "time", we have three distinct "moments": the past, the present, and the future. Of these three "moments", we continually exist in the "present" in what I like to call "The Moment of Now". Because we exist in "The Moment of Now", the "past" is merely a memory of Where We Have Been. The "future", on the other hand, will exist in a later "Moment of Now", yet we can never reach the "future" because we exist in "The Moment of Now".

Because of this, if you choose an affirmation such as "I will receive money tomorrow", you will never receive that money because "tomorrow" never arrives. This is why I mentioned never include the word "will" in your affirmation.

While affirmations based in the (recent) past can be used for affirmations, the strongest affirmation is always based in "The Moment of Now".

Along these lines, a friend of mine recently decided that the safest positive affirmation for him was the simple statement: "I won the lottery". Every night before retiring to bed, he would take a walk to connect with the Universe, lie down in bed, pray, allow his mind to enter Alpha mode, and then silently chant the affirmation "I won the lottery" while visualizing himself cashing in the winning ticket. While his affirmation was based in the "past" (because of the use of the past tense word "won"), his visualization was set in "The Moment of Now".

Within two weeks of starting this ritual, he reported that he had "won the lottery" several times. The problem was, his winning tickets ranged between $2.00 and $50.00... In other words, again, the Universe delivered exactly what he asked for.

But this did not discourage him.

Seeing that the Divinity system worked, he revised his affirmation to: "I am a lottery jackpot winner", and is making preparations of how to spend his winnings.

On a similar note, an acquaintance of mine (we'll refer to as "John") was going through a heavy financial crunch when I showed him the Divinity system. Seeing it and almost instantly grasping it, "John" began silently reciting a positive affirmation each night when he and his wife went to bed. He was using the affirmation "I have lots of money" (which is a very good affirmation to use, especially if your finances are running in or near the red). Having recited the affirmation faithfully – about 20 times a night for nearly two months – John came to me and explained that he had seen some results, but each time there was a positive result, some new financial woe appeared to counteract it.

Through coincidences that had occurred in his life, through watching his children test the Personality Modes, through perceiving matter as energy (and seeing compelling evidence to that effect), he had developed a thorough and unwavering belief in the Divinity system. Yet now, when saying the affirmation with great belief, the Divinity system was producing only minimal results.

John was becoming discouraged.

He was beginning to believe the Universe didn't want – or deem him "worthy" to have money. He thought, perhaps, this was based on some type of Karma.

Going over everything again with John in great detail, we could not find any flaw in his use of the Divinity system. I advised him to keep trying, and together we thanked (not asked, but thanked) God for providing him with an answer.

A week later John returned to me, beaming. He explained that on the very night after his last visit with me, as he went to bed and started his affirmation, his wife sat up and turned on the light. "Lisa" then told him she needed to talk. She went on to explain that, every night when they went to bed she found herself worrying over bills and not having the money to pay those bills. It was keeping her awake at night. She said that she worried over "not having money" off-and-on during the day. Every time the phone rang, she feared it was a bill collector. She was even afraid to get the mail.

Immediately grasping the problem, John had his answer. Inadvertently and unwittingly, Lisa was "counteracting" John's affirmations with those of her own. Because Lisa believed they had "money problems", they had money problems. And because her affirmations were laden with belief they were strong and quickly "delivered".

Understanding the conflict, John then explained the "Divinity system" to Lisa and they began reciting positive affirmations together. Within a week of this, John received a promotion on his job. A tax refund, which was totally unexpected, appeared in the mail. Lisa won a gift certificate for a local grocery. They found an error on their checkbook which added $200.00 to their favor (even though they had both thoroughly examined the checkbook a week before).

I have shared John's story with you to elucidate two key points. First, if you have a partner, you should share this book with them to avoid the counteractive problem experienced by John and Lisa. Second, the successes which followed John and Lisa's ordeal – an unexpected check in the mail, a job promotion, winning a prize, etc. – are good examples of how the Universe "delivers" what you request. The Universe delivers these successes into our lives through natural channels and doorways. It is not "instant" like the matter-producing system. If you want a new Cadillac, and you start reciting the affirmation "I have a new Cadillac", don't jump up each morning and look expectantly at the driveway. A new Caddy is not going to magically appear there unless you use the "instant" process...and that's the hard way to go. More likely, if your affirmation is "I have a new Cadillac", the Universe may deliver in the way of a local car dealership sending you a "pre-approved" loan offer. By taking advantage of this loan offer and buying a new Caddy from the dealer, your affirmation will be fulfilled.

Of course, that's probably not what you wanted, right? You wanted to own a new Caddy. Right?

As I mentioned earlier, your affirmations should be very specific to avoid getting the wrong fulfillment or slant of your affirmation. If you want to own a new Caddy (that's yours, not the bank's), a better affirmation might be: "I own a shiny new red Cadillac Seville, and it's paid for."

Here again, the Universe might initiate the "delivery" by first sending a "pre-approved" loan offer from the local car dealer. And after you have purchased the Caddy, the Universe may continue fulfillment of your affirmation in a "second step", such as by enabling you to win a cash prize or receive some type of financial settlement to pay off the Caddy loan.

During this "two step" fulfillment, you need to continue your affirmation.

To deliver "what you want", the Universe must have doorways to reach you. If you are sitting at home, with no job and very little contact to the outside world, the process will take more time. It will work, but it will take more time than if you are leading an active life.

On the other hand, if you are doing everything in your power to "get what you want" (for the right reasons) − if you're active, receptive, have many open channels and trust in God − you're making it easy for the Universe (God) to deliver what you ask. Success may come very quickly.

As we'll discuss later, after you have started reciting your affirmations, significant "coincidences" can guide you in certain directions and help to open the right channels that allow the Universe's delivery.

Step 5 – Choosing your affirmation.

I would suggest you begin with any one of the following affirmations. Just like walking, it's important to start off one step at a time. As your proficiency in the Divinity system grows, you can move to using multiple affirmations, and thereby "run". But until that point, concentrate on taking small steps, one-at-a-time.

1. "I am happy" – This is the best, the simplest, and the most effective affirmation of all. Why? If you tell the Universe "I am happy", the Universe will provide everything you need to insure that you are, indeed, happy. Whether that's money, love, a new car, career success, good health, or whatever it is that makes you happiest, the Universe will provide. In addition, you can visualize a variety of scenes to reinforce your affirmation. Perhaps you see yourself on the sandy white beaches of some tropical island, or maybe just swinging in a hammock on a sunny afternoon, or mingling with friends at a party. Whatever makes you happy will suffice; the Universe will gladly provide.

As a footnote here, I should mention that there is a curve ball I will be pitching later, regarding the Divinity system and getting "what you want". While it is still premature to discuss this, I'd like you to start examining the "things" that bring you happiness. Is it an abundance of physical belongings, or an abundance of love and joy?

(We'll revisit this, later).

2. "I own lots of money" – When focusing on finances, this is a very effective and practical affirmation. For one reason, if it's

a new Caddy you want, money will allow you to buy it. And you won't have to worry about someone abandoning a 1978 lime green Caddy in your driveway and thereby fulfilling the Universe's delivery. It's also very easy to "visualize" receiving money. Many people I've spoken with accomplish this by visualizing checks arriving in their mailbox. Others imagine themselves making 6-figure deposits into their checking accounts, or imagine looking at their checking register and seeing a 6-figure balance already there.

3. "I am healthy" – This is a very clear and straight-forward affirmation. If you have a health problem you're trying to cure, this is the affirmation for you. While you chant the affirmation, whether out loud or in your mind, simply visualize yourself visiting your physician and being declared healthy. If you have a visible health problem, visualize the ailment gone.

4. "I am loved by the perfect mate for me" – If it's a mate you're looking for, you need to be very careful. As we'll discuss later, it's not always wise to visualize a specific person. You can do it, but there may be unpleasant consequences. For one reason, you would be imposing your will upon that person, and you may find that after you have him/her, they aren't the perfect mate for you after all. Instead of visualizing a specific person, imagine that you are with that perfect mate, but you have your eyes closed (as in being kissed) and do not yet know how they look. Or perhaps you close your eyes and can merely feel their presence next to you. Be receptive, and allow the Universe to deliver.

5. "I own a beautiful home" – Here again, it may be best to use the "I own lots of money" affirmation to help you afford your special home. However, this affirmation works great for helping you find that home as "Step 1" of the home-buying process. I had an acquaintance who became financially able to buy a home after using the "I own lots of money" affirmation for about six months. With her finances prepared, she began

using the "I own a beautiful home" affirmation. She liked Victorian houses, and because her favorite color was blue she visualized a light-blue Victorian when reciting the affirmation. About a month later, while driving to a coworker's house to drop off a briefcase he had forgotten, she turned a corner and saw her dream house exactly as she had pictured it. Moreover, it was currently for sale. And after speaking to the owner, she learned the home was well within her price range. Furthermore, she learned that it had been white, with good paint, but two weeks earlier the owner had capriciously decided to paint it sky blue.

Ironically, her co-worker's briefcase contained the application papers for her loan.

Step 6 – Reciting your affirmation with belief:

Once you have chosen the affirmation that's best for you, all you need to do is state the affirmation to yourself and believe what you are saying. You can either chant the affirmation silently (in your mind), or out loud. The latter is more effective, but either method can produce astounding results. Chant the affirmation for about 5 minutes, visualizing at the same time, then return to normal life and leave the Universe to it's own workings.

While you're "waiting" for the Universe to deliver, it's important that you continue to imagine yourself already owning whatever was requested. Remember: your thoughts are powerful tools. If you recite the affirmations and then start "watching" for the item to be delivered, thinking or wondering when delivery will occur, you're inadvertently thwarting the process by sending the message: "I don't have this item... when will it arrive?"

The best results come by repeating the affirmations daily, and forgetting about them in between. Thank God for what you "want", then leave the details to Him.

Beyond questioning "when" an item may arrive, one major hurdle some people encounter is "belief". For the process to work, you have to wholeheartedly believe that your affirmation is true – and that's not always easy. If a bill collector calls while you're reciting the affirmation "I own lots of money", it can shatter the whole process. That nasty thought – "I don't really have enough money" – is going to flash across your mind. And you will know that as truth. In other words, you'll believe it more strongly than your affirmation.

If your affirmation makes you feel that you're lying to yourself, try adding a "prop" to supplement your belief. For example, if your affirmation is "I own lots of money", but you know your wallet is nearly empty, go out to a novelty store and buy three or four of the fake one-million dollar bills (they're usually available at eBay™). You can then walk around all day thinking: "I've got three-million bucks in my wallet!" And you can believe that, because in effect it is true.

As for "props", if you're after the new Caddy, you might visit the local Caddy dealer and take a picture of the car you want (be sure to ask for the dealer's permission first – if you tell them it's your dream car, they'll most likely oblige). After you have the picture of the Caddy, use scissors to trim the actual Caddy from the picture. Next, go outside and take a picture of your driveway or parking space. When the second picture is developed, affix or superimpose the Caddy so it's sitting in your driveway. You can then frame the picture and place it somewhere frequently seen.

While fake dollar bills, pictures, and other ingenious props can help you achieve your results, you already possess the grandest prop of all: your imagination.

If you're wondering how you can use your imagination, let me provide an example:

When you go to the special place where you meet with God, and begin to recite your affirmations, imagine that you have been transported backward in time by one month. If the date is September 1st, you're going to imagine that the room around you is "how it looked" on August 1st. In other words, what you're seeing as you look around the room is merely an illusion, a memory, or a re-creation. You're looking at the "past" and visiting a Moment of the Past. You "know" that in the real Moment of Now, the room is more abundant, and the bills you had on "August 1st" have all been paid. You also "know" that you currently own all the things you want.

When you end your session, mentally transport yourself back to the "present" date and time and leave your worries in the "past". The "present" day suddenly becomes brighter because it is just that: a present.

Know that when you revisit this space, you will never again return to that "August 1st" level of hardship. Your life is now improving on a minute-by-minute basis. And "tomorrow" – September 2nd – will be brighter than today. Just as August 2nd moved you closer to an improved present.

As we'll discuss in later sections of this book, this game of the imagination isn't far from the truth, because life in effect is an "illusion". Through our collective perceptions, we form the world around us. Every trial and triumph, issue and resolution, malady and cure, are brought about by our own thoughts and perceptions.

Christ tried to teach us this, but we did not learn.

We sit in a chair, knowing it is nothing more than energy, yet it supports us because we believe it will support us.

This same "belief" aspect demonstrates why "superstitions" affect some people and not others. The key is "belief". When a superstitious person is driving down the road and a black cat streaks out in front of them, they might think: "I just crossed the path of a black cat – now I'm going to have bad luck!". And if they deeply believe they will have bad luck, they will have bad luck because they've just rocketed a belief-laden affirmation to the Universe.

The fulfillment of their affirmation (i.e. the car breaks down two blocks later) proffers their belief that superstitions are real, thus creating a cycle.

On the other hand, when the same black cat crosses the path of a non-superstitious person, they think nothing of the incidence, and therefore nothing happens. This proffers that person's belief that superstitions aren't real, but are merely folklore.

By this same way of thinking, the belief aspect can bring about "miracles". We see evidence of this phenomenon at work in any miracle; yet we often fail to recognize the accompanying significance. For example, in Guideposts' Miraculous Healings[11], an anthology of short stories detailing true miracles, we find many appropriate examples. In one such poignant tale, The Gift of Hope, the author recounts the birth of her oldest son (born very ill, placed on life-giving equipment, and not expected to survive). Yet despite the bleak prognosis of the attending neonatologists and pediatricians, the mother refused to give up hope. Instead, she continued to pump and store milk as she "bargained with God" to heal the infant. And some 10 days later, the doomed infant made a miraculous and unexplainable recovery, struggling to free himself from his respirator.

In the same book, a similar story called Touched by Heaven's Hand chronicles a child born with a "large hole between the left and right chambers of his heart". Yet again, despite a grim medical prognosis, the mother refuses to give up hope and tells her child (the affirmation): "Jesus will heal you, little Scotty". She then prays to God: "We believe with all our hearts that You will heal our son". At which time the father says: "I really do believe God is going to heal him." And upon the following medical visit, the hole in Scotty's heart has mysteriously disappeared.

This ability to manifest "miracles" and shape our own lives is our Divinity Factor. Being Divine by default, surrounded by only Divinity, the tools are at hand.

We are not separate from God; we are a part of God; and God is a part of us.

> But thou shalt remember the LORD thy God: for [it is] He that giveth thee power to get wealth, that He may establish His covenant which He sware unto thy fathers, as [it is] this day.

> Deuteronomy 8:18
> The Bible
> KJV

> All things were made by Him; and without Him was not any thing made that was made.
> John 1: 3
> The Bible
> KJV

When can I expect results?

As we discussed earlier, your thoughts are powerful forms of energy. Your belief propels your thoughts. Words and visualization can reinforce and expedite the creative process.

The more you repeat the process and the stronger you believe, the faster you will achieve results.

Let's take that even one step further. If you have shared this book with another family member (such as your spouse), and the two of you are reciting the same affirmation (separately), results will be realized faster. The more people who are involved (and believe), the faster the delivery. (We'll talk more about this in the next section: "collective divinity").

It's important to remember, however, that the Universe needs a "doorway" into your life to "deliver" whatever it is you've requested. You have to be listening for a "knock" at the door. And you need to be willing to get up and answer the door when the Universe comes knocking.

After you've started reciting your affirmations, the first thing that may occur is a "significant" coincidence or other message from the Universe. This is God's way of "ringing the doorbell". It's akin to finding a note from the postman, indicating you have a package that's too large to fit in your mailbox.

Later, we'll look at ways God communicates with us and delivers us these messages. Understanding how these messages fit into the larger picture is an important part of assembling Life's puzzle. It's another one of those "puzzle-piece islands" – and a significant one. However, before we can snap it in place, we need to first interlock some surrounding pieces.

Chapter 15
Collective Divinity

As we've seen, through a combination of affirmations and faith, we can each tap into divinity and create abundancy within our lives. The process begins with a single thought, conceived by a single individual.

As we go about life, we evaluate each significant thought we conceive to determine if the thought is "flawed" or "valid". If we deem the thought as "flawed", we discard it and the divinity process ends there (because we do not believe the thought is correct or true). If, however, we determine our thought is valid and true, we may begin to believe in it. And by doing so, our belief sends this thought hurtling to the "universe" for fulfillment.

Again, "thought" is the tool; "belief" is the force that works that tool.

Now that you understand how the core process works, you may be wondering how your own thoughts can influence broader subjects. For example, how do your thoughts impact matters such as "world peace", "famine", or "disease"?

Suppose, for a moment, that a person who read this book didn't want "a new shiny Cadillac". Suppose, instead, this person had grander aspirations and wanted "world peace"(?). And suppose this same individual began reciting the affirmation: "There is now total world peace".

What impact do you think this affirmation might have?

Could one person's affirmation impact the lives of millions?

To answer this question in terms comprehensible to the human mind, we'll need to make some "earthly" comparisons that might loosely match the corresponding "heavenly" mechanisms. We'll begin this process by looking at what the Universe does when it receives our affirmations or "requests".

As you can imagine, at any given moment the Universe is receiving an incomprehensible amount of "requests" from Earth. While there's really nothing on Earth that compares to this phenomenon, we might liken it to a "giant computerized mail-sorting machine". As the universe receives this "mail" (requests/affirmations) we have hurtled its way, it first sorts these "requests" based on the "priority", which is determined by the accompanying "belief".

In terms we can understand, we might translate this "belief" to the amount of "postage" that was paid. This conveys the "urgency" of the request and is comparable to separating "next-day mail" from 3-day, and 3-day from 5-day, and so on.

After this "mail" is sorted by its priority, it is next sorted by "recipient". That is, the Universe looks at the number of individuals who will be impacted by the fulfillment of any given request. The Universe does not make a "determination" or "judgment" as to whether or not the request will (or won't) be fulfilled – because doing such would thwart our God-given "free will". Instead, it uses a "scoring-like" system we might equate to "checking for correct postage".

For example, to use numbers we can humanly relate to (strictly for the sake of comprehension), let's pretend that a "strong belief" is the equivalent of $1.00 postage and the cost of a "stamp" is also $1.00. If the Universe receives a request from

"Bob Brown" for a shiny new Caddy, and Bob's request contains a "strong belief" ($1.00 postage credit), the Universe will calculate the number of people impacted (we'll say it's just Bob in this example – although that's likely not the case in reality) and determines that Bob has paid sufficient postage. Since Bob has paid the correct postage, the Universe then fulfills his request by creating "coincidences" or "circumstances" that place Bob in the seat of his new Caddy.

In the event that Bob had only included a "moderate" amount of belief (we'll call it 25 cents of postage), the Universe would ignore Bob's request "due to insufficient postage" (belief). If Bob resubmits the same request, and again includes a moderate amount of belief (.25), the universe would continue to "ignore" the request, awaiting the correct "postage".

By doing this, we have a naturally occurring "check and balance" system. This "check and balance" system is in place to prevent us from accidentally getting what we don't really want. You can see why this "check and balance" system exists if you recall our earlier example of the child in the grocery, testing the "Intimidator" personality mode. Such a child might say things such as "I hate you!" or even "I wish you were dead!".

At one time or another, most of us have done this (or something similar). We say or do things we don't really mean. And because of that, the Universe has certain "checks" and "measures" it performs before fulfilling any given request; the prominent "measure" being a necessary saturation of belief.

To look at this from another angle, we might reiterate an earlier example where the disciples were asking Christ why they could not perform miracles (such as curing the boy's mental illness):

And Jesus said unto them: "Because of your unbelief: for verily I say unto you, If ye have faith as a grain of mustard seed, ye

shall say unto this mountain, Remove hence to yonder place; and it shall remove; and nothing shall be impossible to you.
St. Matthew 17:20
The Bible
KJV

Christ's message to us was clear. We can have anything we want (in order to experience). If we can't muster enough belief in this incredibly simplistic principle to actuate it on our own, we need only believe in Him, and He will do it for us:

Just believe it – that I am in the Father and the Father is in me. Or else believe it because of the mighty miracles you have seen me do.
In solemn truth I tell you, anyone believing in me shall do the same miracles I have done, and even greater ones, because I am going to be with the Father.

St. John 14: 11,12
The Living Bible
KJV

Returning to our question of "one person impacting the lives of millions through affirmations", the answer is a definitive "yes" and "no".

How can that be?

To answer that, we'll need to refer back to our "postage" example. In order to bring about such a phenomenal change of world order and impact the lives of millions, this single individual would need to have sufficient belief to "pay" for "postage" of his/her request to every person in the world.

One stamp doesn't cut it – he or she will need billions.

Christ had this abundance of belief (and, of course, still does).

So why hasn't Christ done it?

The answer might shock you:

> We don't want him to.

Why?

As we'll discuss later, our purpose in life is to experience. And in that, we need to know both "good" and "bad". In order to appreciate pleasure, we must know pain. And in order to celebrate joy, we must understand sorrow. To savor sweets, we must have tasted the sour. And so on. This, again, is why the Universe does not "judge" our requests.

By now, you may be wondering how all of this relates to "collective divinity", right?

To set the stage, I needed to present the basics of how the overall system works on a singular basis. While the "postage sorter" might be a bit corny, it allows me to express the fundamentals of how the process works. And now that you can see this, you probably have a good idea how it might also work collectively. But just in case someone hasn't figured it out, we'll look at another example.

Suppose for a moment, that a little girl wanders away from her home, falls into a well, and becomes trapped. And suppose that the ensuing search for this little girl is televised on national news. And as events continue to unfold, and the little girl is discovered (stuck in a well), the emphasis of the new broadcast shifts from "search" to "rescue".

Across the country, you would have people who are praying for the little girl. And as a result of that, the giant "mail sorter" would be receiving thousands of "requests" addressed toward the little girl as "recipient".

The "outcome" of the situation – that is, the final result, or the action(s) the universe might take, is determined by the "polarity" of the requests it receives. This "polarity" is determined by the "expectations" of the senders. In other words, the "giant mail sorter" will receive "mail" from those who "believe" the little girl will be rescued (positive), and from those who "believe" she won't be reached in time (negative).

As the universe receives these requests, it keeps a "running tab" and begins creating circumstances that precipitate the outcome. For example, if the vote is leaning in favor of the little girl's survival (as it likely would be in this scenario), a potent weather system that could hamper rescue efforts might mysteriously "hold off" and baffle meteorologists. By this same measure, favorable "coincidences" may begin to occur, such as a passerby (who just happens to be hauling a backhoe) who stops to aide the rescue effort.

In situations such as this, the Universe may, on rare occasion, use "people" as a tool to bring about resolve – provided the affected individual is willing to become "God's tool". The Universe will not, however, do anything that denies any individual of their "free will". Instead, most often it opts to use "coincidences", "circumstances", or otherwise "unexplainable" events that enable rescue workers to succeed.

The "miracles" brought about by "mass prayer" are an example of this phenomenon at work.

"Rain dances", or other "ceremonies", are similar examples. The difference is that the "recipient" is the "weather" or a particular "issue", rather than a person.

If that statement sent you thinking ahead of the text, good for you.

As we've seen, every thought we "conceive and believe" is hurtled toward the universe and is sorted by "recipient" upon receipt. The whole process begins with a single individual, yet works collectively on a cosmic scale.

Through the course of a normal day, any given individual sends out hundreds of requests. And these requests may include concerns about their personal lives, thoughts about their friends and family, their perceptions regarding the status of their community or country, and even issues facing the larger, general world.

When the recipient happens to be a "thing" (such as weather) or an "issue" (such as world peace, famine, etc.), the universe works in the same manner that it does when the recipient is a "person" (such as the little girl in the well). As the "mail" is received, the universe tallies the "polarities" and continues to manifest "circumstances" that will lead to either victory or defeat, depending on which way the current polarity is indicating. Through this, we can look at any on-going topic (such as world famine) to see if we are growing closer to solving the problem or if we are losing the battle.

The choice is up to us, because our thinking creates the problems we face.

In the highest sense, God's will is our will and our will is God's will.

As you can see, this "universal gear" environment is directly related to one we explored much earlier. Our level of life force turns the gear of our emotional needs. The gear of our emotional needs turns the gear of "mood" or "emotion" (our outlook, and our perceptions of our self and others). As you can now see, this "gear of our mood and outlook" turns the very gear that shapes and defines our circumstances: the gear of our circumstances/environment.

Herein, you have the reasons for always being optimistic and abolishing fear.

The surprise is, these gears are not aligned in a straight row as you may have mentally imagined, but rather in a circle.   As I have mentioned (and will mention again):

All of life is interconnected and occurs in cycles.

It is the "gear of the environment" (you helped to shape) that drives the "gear of your level of life force".

Again:

> Whatever you send out – positive or negative – eventually
> returns to you.

The factors of your personal environment directly influence your level of life force. Your level of life force, first impacts you (through emotional needs), then others (through the PM's), then your personal mood (and attitudes), and finally your community, then your country, and then the world.

In this manner, collective divinity is responsible for the status of every country in the world. And again, it always begins on an individual level. One individual of a species. It all comes down to how a person perceives the status of their country whenever they see the national flag (or something symbolic to them of their country).

As an example, let's say there's a man living in a country where the citizens are oppressed and impoverished. We'll call this man "Abram" for reference. If Abram continually has negative thoughts about his country, due to the atrocities he sees, and therefore thinks affirmations such as "this country is a horrible place to live", unknowingly, he is shaping his own environment by inadvertently using his Divinity. By stating affirmations and believing them, the Universe provides Abram (and his fellow countrymen) with exactly what was requested.

So what can one person do to make life better?

Alone, it is difficult for one person to change the realization created by masses. Even if Abram realizes what he was doing (Divinely) and alters his mode of thinking (to something such as "my country is a great place to live"), the beliefs of others who still think "this is a horrible, famished country" will "outweigh" the beliefs of this one individual.

Abram can, however, make an impact that leads to eventual victory. If he changes his perception about his own environment, and begins to acquire abundance in his personal life, Abram's "neighbors" will witness this abundance and will begin to feel better about the state of their country (albeit a slow and selfish pathway). While this "straight and easy" path is temporarily fulfilling, there is a better way: a lesson Christ showed us.

Think about it.

If you believe in Christ, and believe He could wrought miracles (such as turning water to wine), you likely believe that Christ could have lived in physical abundancy. He could have lived in a resplendent mansion, surrounded by pots of gold and untold riches. And any passersby would have likely listened to whatever Christ was preaching, just as today's man clings to every whisper of Wall street tycoons.

Yet through His wisdom, Christ tried to show a more excellent way. That is, He journeyed meekly from town to town, spreading the message of Hope and Love to raise the collective perception to a positive mode of thinking. He showed how we should strive to overcome our fears and weaknesses (such as the fear of poverty), and place our trust in God, while instilling in the hearts of Mankind. By doing so, Mankind, in turn, could change the polarity of his perceptions, thus creating a better world.

This simple lesson is told and retold throughout the Bible. We can live in abundance by merely requesting whatever we "want" through "prayer" (belief and affirmations). However, before we can live in worriless abundance and tranquility, we need to "preach the gospel" – the message of "Good News" – of hope and love to every living creature". In plain language, we need to educate our fellow man of the power of Love, and the pitfalls of Fear. By doing so, through meeting every stranger with appreciation and acceptance, our own life force grows and is maintained. And simultaneously, by instilling "hope" and "understanding" into the lives we touch – abolishing their fears – we help others improve their own lives and be happier. This, in turn, enables us to live more "worry free". And so on.

When the Biblical prophet Isaiah reached this understanding, and realized how we each have the ability to control our environment and destinies by inspiring "hope" into the "collective", he stated:

1. The Spirit of the Lord God is upon me; because the Lord hath annointed me to preach good tidings unto the meek; He hath sent me to bind up the brokenhearted, to proclaim liberty to the captives, and the opening of the prison to them that are bound.
2. To proclaim the acceptable year of the Lord, and the day of vengeance of our God; to comfort all that mourn.
3. To appoint unto them that mourn in Zion, to give them beauty for ashes, the oil of joy for mourning, the garment of praise for the spirit of heaviness; that they might be called trees of righteousness, the plantings of the Lord, that he might be glorified.
4. And they shall build the old wastes, and shall rise up the former desolations, and they shall repair the waste cities, the desolations of many generations.

Isaiah 61: 1- 4
The Bible
KJV

As we can see in this scripture, Isaiah realized that by preaching hope unto the hopeless, he could break an age-old cycle of negative thinking: "the desolations of many generations".

This basic message, in itself, is the predominant purpose of this book. To better each of our lives, we must strive to better the collective.

> And to love him [God] with all the heart, and with all the understanding, and with all the soul, and with all the strength, and to love [his] neighbour as himself, is more than all whole burnt offerings and sacrifices.
> Mark 12: 33
> The Bible
> KJV

Before we move on, we will look at a few brief examples of how "collective perceptions" shape our communities, countries, and world, with both positive and negative effects.

We'll begin with a brief look at the U.S. If you review U.S. history and consider collective divinity, you can easily see "how" and "why" the U.S. grew to be a rich and powerful nation. It began with our Native Americans, who "set the stage" by deeply appreciating and respecting nature and paying reverence to the land. Columbus then arrived and founded this "bountiful land of milk and honey". And later, after our country was born, we have continued praise through songs such as America, So Beautiful, the National Anthem, God Bless America, and many more. We also pay reverence to our flag (a representation of the country), not only through The Pledge, but also through our "handling" of the flag; folding it in a certain manner, preventing from touching the ground, flying it at half mast when the country mourns. Etc.

Due to these affirmations and thoughts, the USA has grown to be the country it is today. And in this, we see an example of the positive at work. It also sheds insight into why terrorists are so eager to inseminate FEAR into the hearts of Americans.

But now let's look at the other side... a pill that is harder to swallow.

If you were around in the 1960s for the bra-burning sexual rebellion, you've also had a chance to see this phenomenon occur on the "negative" side.

How?

Follow along...

I will, however, preface this section by mentioning that it takes time to accept that we are (collectively) responsible for our own living conditions. This is because we don't want to feel (individually) responsible. We can often be like "Worker A" who does not realize they fear being overweight.

Bear this in mind as you read the following example.

If you take a trip back in time, during the late 1960s we had many "factions" among our society. Each of these factions were advocating their own unique cause. One of the prominent factions here in the U.S. was a group we'll reference to as "the hippies".   Generally speaking, the hippies were the ones attending Woodstock, driving vans garnished with bright flowers, brandishing peace signs, and picketing with posters stating: "Peace" or "Make love not war".

Opposed to this group was "the old-schoolers".   The old-schoolers disapproved of the fun-loving, peace-advocating, marijuana-smoking, and sexually-uninhibited "hippies". To the old-schoolers, national wars were "a matter of country honor and dignity".   And the sexual freedom of the hippies was "incorrigible, promiscuous, and downright disgraceful behavior". This sex was "dirty" and would inevitably lead to disease and unwanted pregnancies.

By the time the mid 1970s rolled around, the beliefs of the old-schoolers were starting to materialize into general society.   In other words, the universe was posting its current "tally" of the leading polarity. It seemed that about every two or three years, a new sexual disease was spreading among the sexually active – each being worse than its predecessor. While not necessarily occurring in this order, there was an influx of genital warts, gonorrhea, herpes, syphilis, hepatitis B, and chlamydia.

Not only was there the influx of these diseases, but a host of new terms were being born. Restroom conversations frequently contained "VD", "The Clap", "crabs", "STDs", or other similar terms. While the old-schoolers were saying: "I told you so", many of the hippies (who had long since merged into society), were tacitly admitting "I guess they were right."

In general, as a society, we began to "expect" these diseases and quietly anticipated the next – expecting it to be worse than its predecessors.

The unspoken fear was:

"What's coming next? When do these diseases stop? Is there no end?"

Collectively, a large part of our society began to believe and anticipate the forth-coming "worst of the worst". Without speaking about it, we were expecting it.

And through this collective belief and anticipation, the disease came to be:

AIDS.

Over a 20-30 year period, we – not just Americans, but people of the world – brought this disease upon ourselves through our thinking. As with all such "deliveries" by the Universe, the disease arrived through what we would perceive as "natural channels"; that is, by "coincidence" something "disturbed" or "awoke" a virus that may have resided dormantly in the jungles since the beginning of time.

Fortunately, though, there is now hope. Just as we brought this disease into being, we can also collectively banish it from existence. As a matter of fact, we are already on the track to finding a cure.

It's important to realize that "collective" goals (such as curing AIDS) are generally accomplished in steps or degrees – not through instant results. When an issue such as AIDS befalls society, we may first be told: "this disease is deadly, epidemic, and presently incurable". As a result, our first reaction is one of great fear. We fear the disease and we fear contact with any unfortunate soul who happens to have the disease.

Fear is the negative polarity.

Again:

> There is no fear in love; but perfect love casteth out fear: because fear hath torment. He that feareth is not made perfect in love.
> 1 John, 4:18
> The Bible

As time passes and education spreads, our fear slowly abates and we begin focusing on the slightly positive. We begin to pity those who are afflicted by the disease and our affirmations change to: "Maybe they'll find a cure – or at least a drug to control the disease".

When more time passes and a larger segment of society is educated, the education banishes a large portion of the fear. Collectively, we become more positive with our thoughts. "The disease can be cured – it's just a matter of time."

161

(As you can see, this process parallels the earlier topic of "forgiveness" and recognizing a fear and appreciating it for what it is).

This latter stage usually brings about the discovery of drugs which slow down the disease. And at this stage, process toward a cure often accelerates.

Why?

When medical researchers announce the discovery and FDA approval of such drugs, the "collective" of society begins to assume: "We will find a cure". Our remaining fear then fades quickly.

As more time passes, and more and more successful drugs are tested and approved, the collective thinking turns to: "A cure is now imminent".

We are currently at this stage with AIDS. And it wouldn't surprise me if, by the time this book reaches print, a cure or inoculation is near.

Ironically, the final stage of the battle is often one in which a "false" cure is found and announced, and a large part of the collective believes "AIDS has been cured" – even if weeks or months later they learn that this miracle cure was actually a failure. That temporary belief of a cure brings about a true cure.

Having said all that, you may be wondering "why haven't we cured cancer?"

The response would be:

1. How many people do you know who, if they found a "lump" in any part of their body, wouldn't automatically "fear" it was cancer?

2. How many people do you know who "believe" we can cure cancer today – not 20 or 30 years from now – but today?

With cancer, we are presently in the "A cure is imminent" stage. And the good news is, a cure will be found.

Why did it take us so much longer to reach this stage?

Think about it...

AIDS is feared, but that fear doesn't impact everyone because not everyone is at risk of contracting the disease. Not all people participate in the sharing of needles, indiscreet sexual activity, or other activities associated with AID's risk. Cancer, on the other hand, is indiscriminate and can strike anyone at any time – quite unexpectedly. It's an ambush disease. Therefore, the fear associated with cancer is considerably stronger and more difficult to overcome.

This fear lives on.

People walk around every day fearing they might have an undiscovered form of cancer.

Due to all the hard work by our medical researchers, as screening procedures continue to improve, and new drugs are released to slow and combat the deadlier cancers, our fear will abate. And once that occurs, and we begin to think more positively, a cure will follow.

As one last mention on collective divinity, Christ provided us with many examples and lessons about how the Divinity process works: both singular and collectively. These are especially prominent in Matthew chapters 8 and 9.

Below, I've included a few verses from Matthew 9, using the Revised Standard version to ease interpretation. Read closely and see how many you find:

(18) While he [Christ] was thus speaking to them [some disciplines], behold, a ruler [the rabbi of a local synagogue] came in and knelt before him, saying, "My daughter has just died; but come and lay your hand on her, and she will live." (19) And Jesus rose and followed him, with his disciples. (20) And behold, a woman who had suffered from a hemorrhage for twelve years came up behind him and touched the fringe of his garment; (21) for she said to herself, "If only I touch this garment, I shall be made well." (22) Jesus turned, and seeing her he said, "Take heart, daughter; your faith has made you well." And instantly the woman was made well. (23) And when Jesus came to the ruler's house, and saw the flute players, and the crowd making a tumult, (24) he said, "Depart; for the girl is not dead but sleeping." And they laughed at him. (25) But when the crowd had been put outside, he went in and took her hand, and the girl arose. (26) And the report of this went all through the district.

Matthew 9:18-26
The Bible
Revised Standard Edition

If you read the text closely, you may have noted three specific examples of the divinity process at work in this brief text. The "singular" example relates to the "woman suffering from a hemorrhage", who stated the affirmation: "If I only touch his garment, I shall be made well." At which time Christ turned to her and said: "Take heart, daughter, your faith has made you well".

While it is unclear whether or not the woman comprehended the divinity process, Christ conveyed it to her through his selection of words. You will note that Christ did not say: "I have made you well" or "God has made you well", but instead attributed "faith" as the catalyst. By doing so, he demonstrated to the woman that she need not "touch his garment" for healing, but could do so through faith and love of God, at any time.

The "collective" example here was started by the ruler (the Rabbi), who came to Christ stating the affirmation: "My daughter has just died; but come and lay your hand on her and she will live." At this point, Christ might have treated this situation like the other, and said: "Your faith has made your daughter live again". At which time the daughter might have returned to life. However, you will note that Christ did not do this, and treated one situation differently than another.

Why?

To understand this, we must mentally transport ourselves back in time to the day Christ walked the Earth. In Christ's era, there was no separation of "state and church". Any "governments" that existed were powerless shells, and the laws of the land were set forth and enforced by priests, clergy, or other such deities of the church. If you read the Living Bible version of Matthew 9:18, you will see that this "ruler" is referred to as a "Rabbi"; if you read the same verse using the Revised Standard or King James version, the "Rabbi" is referred to as a "ruler". This is because, in Christ's day, these two words were largely interchangeable.

In today's mode of thinking, when we envision Christ going to a Rabbi's home, we might envision Christ and the Rabbi going to a quiet, modest bungalow with a dirt floor and straw thatched roof. However, because the "rabbi" was a "ruler", Christ wasn't expecting a such a humble abode. Instead, a ruler would likely live in a palace swarming with "flute players", "servants" and "crowds". And because of the presence of these onlookers, it was likely that the daughter's death was known and believed by those at the Rabbi's home. That would make the issue one of "collective" divinity.

So what did Christ do upon arriving at the ruler's house?

He told the crowd: "Depart (Go away!). For the girl is not dead but sleeping."

For someone who does not comprehend the divinity process, Christ's statement might seem somewhat illogical. After all, in order to edify God, wouldn't it be better to have a crowd of witnesses?

Some Christians will defend this by saying "no", that the Bible teaches us that such displays in public are "the work of vanity", and spiritual matters (such as fasting or speaking in tongues), should be kept between God and Man. This, however, starts a chain of contradictions with other Biblical scriptures, in which Christ openly performed miracles in the midst's of crowds (and instructed his followers in this manner).

Secondly, why would Christ say: "The girl is not dead, but sleeping"? Couldn't this be viewed as a lie? Wouldn't it be in Christ's (or God's) better interest to have a doctor of the day pronounce the daughter as soundly dead instead of claiming she was merely sleeping? Wouldn't such an action add validity to the miracle?

A Christian friend of mine suggested that perhaps the girl wasn't actually dead, but was comatose and thus "sleeping". He stated that perhaps her heartbeat and breathing rate had dropped to imperceptible levels, fooling the Rabbi and spectators. While this is a feasible possibility, it comes across as stretch. It also leaves Christ's "Depart!" statement as a bit of a mystery.

If you understand the divinity process, however, the purpose for both of Christ's statements should be clear. Christ realized that he could "activate" the ruler's affirmation by "laying his hand upon the daughter". Christ also knew the "flute players" and the "crowd" had already formed their own beliefs. And since some of them had "seen" the daughter dead (seeing is believing), their belief would be very pure and strong. In other words, in that "mailer sorter" in the sky, the belief of the Rabbi would be weighed against the beliefs of the onlookers.

In one fell swoop, Christ weakened the crowd's belief by planting a seed of doubt. Due to his statement, some of the crowd may have immediately doubted their own assumption, wondering if the daughter might indeed be asleep. And moreover, Christ planted this doubt while telling them to "depart", thus preventing the crowd from reaffirming any belief with second glances and evaluations.

As a footnote, I'd like to add that Christ certainly had sufficient faith to overcome the beliefs of the crowd. However, by handling the situation as He did, He enabled the Rabbi's faith to be that healing catalyst -- just as he had with the woman. Whether or not Christ proffered the Rabbi's belief with His own is a question that may never be answered. The principles remain the same. And through this example, we were rewarded with an insightful lesson to help us understand the collective process.

Chapter 16
How We Learn

Okay. It's time for a subject change so we can move on.

The next puzzle-piece we'll be snapping in place relates to how we each learn things differently and become distinctly unique. As an example, we'll look at a parable I've dubbed The Stove. It's one we'll refer back to later in this text, so bear that in mind as you read.

The Stove:

In the 1960's, when Tom was age 5, he enjoyed helping his mother in the kitchen. As she went about her cooking, Tom was fascinated that she could make treats (like cookies or cake) from basically nothing except a little sugar, flour, a mix of spices, and water.

In addition to the wonderful foods and smells of the kitchen, Tom found many of his mother's tools and appliances fascinating. He especially liked their gas stove, and loved watching when his mother turned on a burner and a flame would spring up and dance around the circle.

From past experience, Tom knew the flames were hot. So therefore, when he came in one day to find his mother preparing to cook at a new electric stove – which had no flames – Tom was confused at how the stove could work without fire. As a matter of fact, he soon became convinced it couldn't work.

With no fire, there was no heat, right?

"Look at this, Tom," his mother said, "I bought a brand new stove today. Isn't it great?"

Tom looked skeptically at the stove. "It doesn't have any fire. How can it be hot without fire?"

Tom's mother grinned. "This stove doesn't use gas to make fire, Sweetie. It's a new kind that works with electricity."

Tom still wasn't convinced. He was sure that poor ole' mom had been bamboozled by some suave appliance salesman. And knowing that a burner couldn't be hot without fire, he decided he'd have to break mom's delusion by proving her wrong. Reaching up, he started to touch one of the burners, but his mother quickly grabbed his hand and pulled it away.

"Don't touch that burner, Tom. It's hot," his mother chided. "You'll get burned, and we don't want you to get burned."

Determined to prove Mom wrong, Tom looked her defiantly in the eye and slapped his hand on the glowing burner."

The purpose of this parable is very simple. It helps us to see how we each learn lessons differently from our life experiences. When making a mistake such as the one Tom made, some of us would emerge learning only that: flames aren't the only things that are hot.

Others might also gain from this experience that burns really hurt.

Others might walk away learning that, at the ripe old age of 5, mom still may be a little wiser than we are.

And still others might also learn that Mom may have our best interest at heart, and it's a good idea to listen to her.

As you can see, if two identical children were to undergo this same experience, and one child walks away learning only that "burns hurt", while the second walks away learning "Mom may still be a little wiser than we are " and "Mom may have our best interest at heart", the two children would no longer be identical and would regard the next experience with different points of view. When this is compounded by different children having different experiences and learning different lessons from each experience, the result is children who are very unique, with disparate points of view about any given subject.

How We Learn and What We Know – the sum of our experiences – are what determines Who We Are. It is these differences that work together to shape our lives and make each of us unique individuals.

Just like little Tom concluded "with no fire, the stove couldn't be hot", most of our erroneous decisions come from what we think we know (and don't really know at all).

Life works in this same manner. Because only a portion of our life puzzle is assembled and we can't see the full picture, we end up making erroneous assumptions. We think that power and money can guarantee our happiness, when we already have the ability to live in bliss. We think that the world around us is physical and solid, when in fact it is completely malleable to our will. We think that we must suffer disease, when our own thinking is the exact cause for these afflictions. We think of our calamities as "strokes of bad luck" or fate, when they are merely consequences of our own decisions. We think, if our marriage requires work to succeed, we must have the wrong partner.

We are a species plagued with misconceptions.

Our challenge is to overcome.

At all given times, God is with you, willing to communicate with us through intuitions and feelings. The problem is, based on our existing flawed foundations of knowledge, we often view His messages as "illogical". We follow our mind over our feelings and thus shut God out of our life. We beg for His guidance, yet refuse to accept it when provided.

To escape this trap we've created, we must open up to "new possibilities" or "new foundations of thinking". And to accomplish this feat, we must first "unlearn" our perception of the world, then "relearn" it correctly, as you are doing now.

We must also learn Why We Are Here.

Chapter 17
Our Purpose in Life

"The human mind is not capable of grasping the Universe. We are like a little child entering a huge library. The walls are covered to the ceilings with books in many different tongues. The child knows that someone must have written these books. It does not know who or how. It does not understand the languages in which they are written. But the child notes a definite plan in the arrangement of the books – a mysterious order which it does not comprehend, but only dimly suspects."[12]

Albert Einstein

What is our purpose in life? Why are we here? What is our goal?

As I mentioned earlier, there is a reason we each individually arrive at these questions at some point during our lives. In the upcoming section on reincarnation, we'll be looking at that specific reason. However, at this point of our journey, discussing why we arrive at this question would still be premature. Instead, we'll look at the predominate questions themselves for insight.

To truly answer questions such as "What is our purpose in life", we must first stop placing ourselves at the question's center. This is because, by placing ourselves as the focal point, we are separating and distinguishing ourselves from God and the collective. This is the equivalent of your hands detaching themselves from your body, then turning and asking you: "What is my purpose in life?". At which time you might answer: "Your purpose is to be my hands! I need you so I can grasp, and hold, and touch, and feel. Now get back on my arms!"

God needs us for the same reasons. Our purpose in life is to experience all that can be experienced. And through doing such, we increase the sum of "God": the collective.

But let's pause for a moment and look at this in another light. In the parable of The Stove, Tom's mother used the stove to "create" through baking. Whenever we bake a pie or build a snowman or make anything, we are creating. With that in mind, you need only ask yourself "Why do I create?"

We create so we can experience and appreciate what we've created.

Experience is the ultimate teaching tool. It is "all there is to live for". It is the sole purpose for life, and the soul purpose for living.

God made us – and everything – for that exact reason: so He could create and experience through His creation of "the All and the Everything".

Let's look at this from one other angle...

Going back to Merriam-Webster's definition of "knowledge", "knowledge" is defined as:

"understanding gained by actual experience (a ~ of carpentry); something learned and kept in the mind."

This gives birth to a question: "If knowledge is based on 'understanding gained by actual experience', how can anyone become 'all-knowing'?"

There is only one answer. We have to be everything. To understand every aspect and every experience of every life form, you must be each life form.

There is no other way.

As we've covered — through energy — God is all things. Simultaneously.

How else could He be "all-knowing", "omnipresent", and "all powerful"?

The problem is, the term "all-knowing" is like infinity. It stretches beyond the limitations of our mind and leaves us wondering what does "all-knowing" include? Are there limitations? Does God know how a tree feels when it is chopped down? Does He know how a dog feels when it's petted? Or how a blade of grass feels when it basks in the summer sun?

Of course He does!

How?

Because God is all things (through energy). And because of that, He is "all-knowing" without limitation. We (the "life forms") are a part of God (the collective). We are made from God, by God, and are an intrinsic part of God.

If a new life form — some type of amoeba never studied before — is born at this moment on Mars, God simultaneously experiences the birth of this new life form because "He Is All Things". And through this experience, the acquired knowledge instantly becomes included in the: "Tree of Knowledge".

As was done in Genesis, I use the term "Tree of Knowledge" for its symbolism. Like a tree, knowledge has a main trunk and several

175

branches. And from each of these branches sprout lesser branches. These lesser branches sprout even lesser branches, eventually giving way to stems, leaves, and fruit. And while the branches, sprigs, fruit, and leaves are each constructed differently, they are each "part of the whole". Collectively, the sum of the parts determines the sum of the whole.

Likewise, the overall "collective" principle works in this same harmonic fashion. The collective is comparable to a "tree". It is constructed of people, plants, animals, and a host of other life-forces that are each different in shape and design. And just like the leaves of a tree exist to gather sunlight, and the roots exist to draw moisture, every part of the tree has a specific and unique purpose for existing. Moreover, every part of the tree is essential for the tree's growth and betterment.

Returning to our question ("what is our purpose in life"), the answers should now be clear. God put us here so, through us – as part of the collective – He (we) could experience. And moreover, He made us all different to widen the dragnet. Through these differences, He can experience all extremes (or moderations between) at the same time. Through us, He can experience good and bad, sadness and happiness, pain and ecstasy, and everything imaginable.

We are the grandest experience of all.

Why?

Because we are made in God's image; that is, we can also create. And through us, He can experience our experience of creating.

Our purpose in life is simpler than you might expect: we are to experience all that we can experience. By doing so, we increase the composition of "all-knowing". We, in fact, "praise God" in the highest sense through living. We add to the whole of the sum.

He has given us the tools to experience anything we desire. He has also encouraged us to use these tools. The next step is up to us.

Putting this more simply, our mission here on Earth is to:

1. Create
2. Experience and appreciate what we have created.
3. Give our creation away (so that others who have not yet learned to create their own abundance can experience and appreciate it), and then restart the cycle.

"Need" does not exist:

Whoa!!! Wait a minute... Give it away? What? Are you kidding? How can I live abundantly if I am giving away everything I have?

I thought that one might catch you off guard. And no, beyond the initial price of this book, you will not be asked to "give" to myself or the publisher. So let me explain...

This is the curve ball I mentioned earlier.

True abundance can only be obtained in a spiritual sense. Regardless of how much you create; regardless of how many "things" you stockpile and store away, you will never acquire lasting happiness from any possession.

So why did we bother learning the steps to create? Was that a waste of time?

By all means, no. It was a necessary lesson for a thorough understanding of how the process works. It is also a tool which you can still use to acquire "things" to experience.

The problem most people face is, the only way they can actually learn is through their own experience. If someone tells you "the stove is hot", depending upon who tells you this, you may or may not opt to believe them. This is because:

Experience is the only truth or real thing in life; everything else is hearsay.

My telling you "the stove is hot" can, in no way, ever compare to your laying your hand upon the burner. And for some of us, we must be "burned" in order to learn.

I think it's safe to say that most of our society follows the bumper-sticker philosophy: "He who dies with the most toys, wins". We believe that we need certain "things" to provide us with happiness. For example, those who live in the inner-cities might say: "If I only lived in suburbia, had a nice home, and drove one of those mega-sized SUV's, I'd be happy. All the people living in suburbia are happy."

Yet upon arriving in suburbia, owning a new home, and purchasing a SUV, they find that happiness still eludes them. It lies "someplace else". It now becomes: "If I only lived in the wealthier part of town, had a larger house, and drove a Lexus, I'd be happy. All the people in the richer parts of town, who drive a Lexus, are happy."

Yet upon arriving at the richer part of town, happiness, again, has vacated and now resides in Malibu.

"If I only lived in Malibu or someplace exotic, with an in ground pool and a yacht, and could trade my Lexus for a Porsche or a Rolls, I'd be happy. Everyone who lives in Malibu and has a swimming pool and a Rolls is happy."

Yet upon arriving in Malibu or West Palm Beach, guess what?

"If I only lived on some exotic island – or had two houses, one in West Palm Beach and one on Saint Thomas, then I'd be truly

178

happy. That's what it takes."

And the cycle goes on.

The more we have, the more we want: bigger and better and better.

We tell ourselves: "I need these things to be happy" Yet once we get whatever "thing" we hoped for, we find we are soon not happy at all.

This problem stems from Man's erroneous perceptions. We are raised and taught that certain "needs" exist, and we "need" certain things to be happy. Man teaches us "there is never enough" and "things come in limited quantities". And therefore, we must gather and hoard as many things as we can so we will never "need".

Yet after you have learned to create, you realize that Man's perception here is quite wrong. You also realize that Man inadvertently "creates" shortages through his collective thinking. In addition, you learn that material "things" suddenly lose their appeal once you learn to create, because – once you can create any "thing" at will – "things" suddenly become burdens. After all, what is the value of hoarding "things" when you can create, and recreate, multiple copies at will? A man with lots of things is suddenly no "richer" or "better" than a beggar; because the beggar can create an equal amount of "things" at will. In other words, in God's eyes, "all men are created equal". Whether you were born "rich" or "poor", or became either during your life, is immaterial.

Once you have learned this lesson, you spiritually ascend by realizing that God will fulfill all of your needs – and therefore, "need" does not exist.

The only real need that has ever existed is our need to connect with God. So long as you love God, and thank Him for what you have, every other "need" ceases.

Jesus tried to impress this lesson to us and we haven't listened. He told us:

Lay not up for yourselves treasures upon earth, where moth and rust doth corrupt, and where thieves break through and steal: But lay up for yourselves treasures in heaven, where neither moth nor rust doth corrupt, and where thieves do not break through nor steal:
Matthew 6:19,20
The Bible
KJV

He also told us:

Therefore I say unto you, Take no thought for your life, what ye shall eat, or what ye shall drink: nor yet for your body, what ye shall put on. Is not the life more than meat, and the body than raiment?
Behold the fowls of the air: for they sow not, neither do they reap, nor gather [store] into barns; yet your heavenly Father feedeth them. Are ye not much better than they?
Matthew 6: 25,26
The Bible
KJV

Our monks and rabbis – those of the Spiritual Personality Mode – already know this.

"Need" does not exist as we imagine it. In effect, "Need" is a concept of Man, based on Man's fears.

Failure:

As another example of Man's erroneous thinking, Man teaches us "we can fail". The concept of "failure" is based on fear, and is another flawed mode of thinking.

180

"Failure" is no more than a matter of perception.

As you now know, our purpose in life is to experience. If you participate in a contest and "fail" or "lose", yet walk away having learned from the experience, did you indeed "fail"?

"Right" and "Wrong" are other examples of Man's flawed thinking. These misnomers stem from our "need" for love and appreciation. Yet true love is completely unconditional. When we unconditionally love someone, they are free to do whatever they choose. They can do no "right" or "wrong".

Yet when Man first experienced "love", it was so precious he feared its loss. Therefore, in a feeble attempt to control — a "greed" for love — Man applied the terms "right" and "wrong" to behavior. He said, "if you love me, you will do this because it is 'right'", and "if you love me, you won't do this because it is 'wrong'". In other words, Man conditionalized the unconditionable and created the grandest oxymoron of all time: conditional love.

As a final note, before we move on, we'll look at one more point related to our life mission of experiencing.

Throughout this text, I have often mentioned that God gave Man "free will". This subject, however, runs much deeper than many people realize. As demonstrated symbolically through the Biblical story of Adam and Eve, God created Man and then placed him in a "safe-haven" of sorts. That is, Man was placed in "The Garden of Eden", a paradise whereas he would never be forced to experience (or "need").

After placing Man in this sanctuary, God presented Man with a simple choice. In other words, because of His unconditional love and because He had given Man true free will, God warned Man that if he ate from a certain tree, Man would experience "good and evil"; that is: toil and hardship, death, famine, disease (etc.).

Without reciting the entire text of Genesis chapters 2 and 3, when Eve saw this tree she saw that "...the tree was good for food, and that it was pleasant to the eyes, and a tree to be desired to make one wise".

The purpose of this colorful and symbolic tale is to impress that we were given a choice. Upon our creation, we chose to experience and "taste the fruit" of the "Tree of Knowledge of Good and Evil". We chose to become a proactive part of God, in the pursuit of achieving all that could be achieved, and learning all that can be learned.

Chapter 18
Everlasting Existence

In the previous two chapters, we focused on three subjects that share a common thread. We began with The Stove Parable, and learned:

>Experience makes us Who We Are.

Next, we looked at "knowledge", and learned:

>Experience also determines What We Know.

And third, we looked at our Life Mission, learning:

>Experience is Why We Are Here.

Like the egg, with three parts being one, we can define this cosmic egg of "Egg-perience" as:

>1. Who We Are
>2. What We Know
>3. Why We Are Here

Now that you understand this, you can remove the questioning word "What?" from these statements and re-arrange them to boldly declare:

>We Know Who We Are and Why We Are Here

But let's simplify this one step further...

Through Life experiences, we earn knowledge.

Most shortly said, we: Learn.

Worded in another manner, since our purpose in life is to experience:

We Exist To Learn

Or:

To Learn, We Exist

Or more insightfully:

To Learn We Exist

Collectively, our mission is: To Learn We Exist.

Since we have already explored the "We" portion of this statement by discussing "the collective", and have also discussed the "To Learn" portion by discussing "experience", we'll be moving on to the final component: "Exist".

Like any of our "cosmic eggs", the egg of "Existence" has three parts – each of which can be viewed separately, yet each of which are required for the whole to be complete.

We'll start by looking at the first of these three components: Life.

The Egg "Shell": Life

To begin our discussion on life, let's look back at our Life Puzzle.

For most of you, whenever I've mentioned your "Life's puzzle", you've likely visualized a "picture puzzle" that was partially assembled, lying on a flat surface. If that's the case, we're going to give that mental image a big "twist".

From this point on, instead of imagining your puzzle being flat and framed, think of it as round – that is, shaped like a globe of the world. By doing this, as the frames and borders mentally dissolve, the previously "unconnected" becomes connected.

For example, let's suppose that while your puzzle was "flat", you were mentally using "birth" as the left border and "death" as the right border. As you "wrap" your puzzle around the globe, "birth" and "death" become nothing more than a line. A meridian of sorts; a Greenwich "Time Line".

This "frameless" mode of thinking is truer to reality because:

Life has no borders.

And, as we've seen:

All aspects of Life occur in cycles and are interconnected.

The problem we face again is one of Mans' erroneous perceptions that we've been taught throughout life. Man tends to view Life as a "lineal" event, rather than as a "non-ending cycle". He sees life as an event "beginning" at birth, "ending" at death, and spanning calendar dates from "A" to "Z".

This "lineal" thinking, however, presents us with an obvious conflict. As we look at the world around us, we see non-changing cycles in virtually everything except life. Life is like the one person at a red shirt convention, who happens to be dressed in blue. It stands apart, and therefore seems all the more curious.

When we look at the universe, we see certain harmonic patterns which are each in some way interconnected. Our ocean's tides rise and fall, in conjunction with the moon. The moon passes through a never-ending cycle, ranging from "new", to "half", to "full". While this occurs, the earth and moon revolve around the sun, giving birth to our four primary seasons. These seasons come and go, continuously renewing our planet, helping to ensure the cycles will continue.

Our females are well aware of the 28-day reproductive cycle, and our animals follow a similar cycle we tamely call "heat" or "coming into season". The gestation period of every mammal follows yet another cycle, which blends congruently to-and-from the "gears" of reproduction — just like winter gives way to spring, night turns to day, or the tides rise and fall in the "gears" of season.

Our insects and "lower" animals follow specific patterns in their own growth, evolving from larva to adult; caterpillar to butterfly; tadpole to frog.

Parasites follow their own cycle when interacting with their host. And diseases, which are often forms of parasites, follow "stages" of their own.

We are submersed in a world of cycles, yet despite our acknowledgment of these cycles, Man continues to view life as a lineal, single-occurrence event.

This might be compared to Early Man's perception of Earth, in the days when the world was perceived as "flat", prior to Columbus's epic voyage. Despite the visible indications that the world might indeed be round (such as the bending of the ocean horizon, or the shapes of the sun and moon), Man somehow knew the Earth was "lineal". He then set out to prove himself right (dispel the fear of being wrong) by designing a full astrology system that demonstrated how the universe — the sun, the constellations, and planets — revolved around Earth: the universe's center. The problems arose, however, when certain pieces of the puzzle didn't quite fit. And when this occurred, Man either forced them into place, discarded them as flawed, or laid them aside while awaiting new data.

In this example, we can see how Man's errors in the past (such as perceiving the world as flat and "lineal") mimic the errors he is repeating today (by viewing life as lineal). This, in itself, is yet another cycle.

In today's world, Man desires to view life as a "lineal" occurrence. Self-assured of this, he has set out to prove himself right by chronicling history and recording the "lives" of fellow man in lineal standards. In our books, in our obituaries, and on tombstones, human lives are portrayed in lineal terms. Man chisels an inscription on a tombstone ("Here lies John Doe, Jan 1, 1900 - December 31, 1999") and then turns to fellow man and boldly declares:

"See... life is lineal. It's written there, and that proves it."

By that same token, Man discards the pieces that don't neatly fit into his puzzle. For example, our "spiritual mediums" — those who can communicate with the "dead" — are often deemed as "scam artists" or "nut-cases". And those who claim having "life-after-death" or "near-death experiences" are met with the same disdain. As are those who say they have seen ghosts. This is because Man cannot correlate or reconcile these phenomena with his lineal perception of life. He is so determined to prove himself right, he often overlooks "the shapes of other planets" — the cycles around us.

187

Like Columbus' voyage, it will take a monumental event to shake Man awake. An event, such as Christ's return to Earth.

I tell you now, the only flaw is Man's perception. Uniform with everything around us, life is a cycle, harmonizing with all other aspects of the universe. And like the shell of an egg, life is empty without the accompanying components.

Let's imagine for a moment:

Suppose for a moment, that you could transport yourself into outer space, at a fixed position overlooking the planet Earth. And suppose, as you watch the Earth from this "heavenly" perspective, you can see it slowly turning on its axis. The features − continents, mountain ranges, snowcaps, and oceans − continually appear on the horizon, pass by, and then disappear around the opposite horizon.

As you continue to watch this rotation, you realize that with each passage of the Greenwich time line, another day on Earth has come and gone.

Now let's modify this journey by imagining that instead of looking at the Earth, you are looking at your own life puzzle, spinning upon it's axis. Again, from your "heavenly" perspective, you can see how certain aspects of the puzzle are separate, yet are each a part of the whole. The "puzzle-piece islands" − the issues we face − those "continents and land masses" of Life's puzzle, are connected by the "oceans of life" and "straits" leading to other continents. And without these land masses, life would have no feature or structure.

Life, in a sense, would be how many view death: a vast wasteland of nothingness.

The Egg Yolk: Death

"There is no death. There are no dead. Reformation is never
denied us, here or hereafter."
Tompkins and Bird
The Secret Life of Plants[13]

Death, in a true and permanent sense, is another example of Man's
flawed thinking.

Why?
Because death cannot and does not exist.

As we have discussed, God is all things. He is every stone, every
plant, every blade of grass, and everything you encounter. And in
that, He has always been and will always be. He is "energy",
constantly changing shape and form.

Because of this, the terms "life" and "death" are both misnomers.
Since death is impossible, there is really no "life". Instead, there
is merely existence.

Most simply put: "I am".

This includes:
"I have been."
"I am."
"I always will be".

Yet another "cosmic egg", with three parts that equal one whole.

Rather than view life as the "beginning" and death as the "end" –
or perceive life as being "aware" and death as "unaware" – we need
to modify our perceptions. "Life" is the state in which our soul –
life force – is operating inside a physical host (our body) in a
physical environment. "Death" is the transference of this energy

189

from the physical realm to the spiritual on "the other side". "Reincarnation" is the transference from the "spiritual" back again into the "physical".

We might compare the process of "death" to sunlight hitting a window. As light passes through a pane of glass, a portion of that light is converted to heat, while another portion remains as light.

When we "die" – that is, when our light shines upon the window of death – our soul and consciousness pass through, while the physical body remains physical.

And just like heat can escape back through the glass and create wind, due to its rising, we too can return to "life" in other forms.

By default, being part of The Collective, we have always been and will always be. And that being the case, death, in a permanent form, is impossible.

If you're beginning to grasp and accept being a part of The Collective, it should be easy for you to disregard "death" as a misnomer. This is because, if one part of the collective were to literally "die", the whole collective would cease to exist through "death" becoming a reality. In other words, to admit death could exist is to admit that "God" – any part of The Collective – could die.

This is the primary lesson Christ tried to show us through his visit on Earth. Death is not the final "end of ends" and is overcome. It is merely a change; existence has and will continue.

"And Jesus said unto him [the thief on the cross who asked Christ remember him], 'Verily I say unto thee, Today thou shalt be with me in paradise'."
Luke 23:43
The Bible
KJV

Having said this, I'd like to present a question for you to ponder:

Since medical science can neither prove nor disprove the "end" of life, which way does the evidence lean? How much evidence exists to prove life simply "ends" at death, versus the indications that life goes on?

If you've ever seen the television show Crossing Over (with John Edward), its probable you've seen evidence of "life after death" and already believe. As a medium connecting those who have crossed with those who are still here, John does a wonderful job of compassionately relaying messages. Often, the messages John delivers to those who are still here are so incredibly personal and arcane that true mediumship is the only possible explanation. In many instances, the messages describe experiences that occurred while the "living" person was completely alone – experiences that were not witnessed by anyone except the involved person, with no means through which John (or a member of his crew, family member, etc.) could have possibly known.

If you don't receive Crossing Over in your local area, Mr. Edward has several books available recounting his experiences, as do many other renowned mediums, such as James Van Praagh (Talking to Heaven).

Herein, through connecting with "those who have crossed", we see yet another part of our life puzzle coming together. On one side of our "global" puzzle, we have the interchange of life force occurring among the "living"; on the opposite side, beyond the "Greenwich time line" of Life, we have "those who have crossed". Yet by understanding how "attention" can cause the exchange of life force, we can begin to understand how mediumship works. We look at our life puzzle, and see how a "continent" on one side of the globe is connected with a "continent" on "the other side", in a "day" which has not yet occurred.

Referring back to an earlier example we looked at, if your mother is in another state, and she thinks about you and decides to call, her name may "pop into your head" when your subconscious picks up and recognizes the stream of inbound life force. This same principle holds true between "the living" and "those who have crossed". If someone on the "other side" begins thinking about you, their name — "memory" as we wrongly put it — may "pop into your head". And by this same token, they may even speak to you in the "Universal" language, sending you images, emotions, or sounds to convey a message.

By being "in tune" with these "transmissions", a medium can connect you to "those on the other side".

I tell you now, you do not need a medium for this to occur. You need only "open yourself" to communication, and "pay attention" to the subtle messages you see.

In other books, besides those by Mr. Edward and Mr. Van Praagh, you can find the personal recounts of those who have returned from death in what we call Near Death Experience (NDE). Authors such as Dannion Brinkley (At Peace in the Light) and Betty J. Eadie (Embraced by the Light) both tell of their own NDEs in very vivid detail.

The process of Death:

In the book Life After Life[14], author Raymond A. Moody, Jr., M.D., takes a slightly different approach for explaining NDE's by interviewing numerous "survivors". In his book, he notes several common experiences described by those who "die" and are brought back. On pages 21-23, Moody summarizes these common elements into one basic model.

I've included this model because I find it worthy of sharing here. Not only is it informative, but it also touches on information we'll be exploring in the next chapter.

The Near-Death Account:

"A man is dying and, as he reaches the point of greatest physical distress, he hears himself pronounced dead by his doctor. He begins to hear an uncomfortable noise, a loud ringing or buzzing, and at the same time feels himself moving very rapidly through a long dark tunnel. After this, he suddenly finds himself outside of his own physical body, but still in the immediate physical environment, and sees his own body from a distance, as though he is a spectator. He watches the resuscitation attempt from this unusual vantage point and is in a state of emotional upheaval.

After a while, he collects himself and becomes more accustomed to his odd condition. He notices that he still has a "body", but one of a very different nature and with very different powers from the physical body he has left behind. Soon other things begin to happen. Others come to meet him and to help him. He glimpses the spirits of relatives and friends who have already died, and a loving, warm spirit of a kind he has never encountered before – a being of light – appears before him. This being asks him a question, nonverbally, to make him evaluate his life and helps him along by showing him a panoramic, instantaneous playback of the major events of his life. At some point he finds himself approaching some sort of barrier or border, apparently representing the limit between earthly life and the next life. Yet, he finds that he must go back to earth, that the time of his death has not yet come. At this point he resists, for by now he is taken up with his experiences in the afterlife and does not want to return. He is overwhelmed by intense feelings of joy, love, and peace. Despite his attitude, though, he somehow reunites with his physical body and lives.

Later he tries to tell others, but he has trouble doing so. In the first place, he can find no human words adequate to describe these unearthly episodes. He also finds that others scoff, so he stops telling other people. Still, the experience affects his life profoundly, especially his views about death and its relationship to life."

Chapter 19

The Egg White: Reincarnation

Okay. Let's play a game with our imagination again and pretend that we've died. What do you think happens after we've floated down that proverbial "tunnel of light"?

Do our souls enter some state of "sleep", awaiting Judgment Day to arrive?

Are there friends and relatives waiting to greet us on the "other side"?

And if so, what happens next?

Do you suppose we then just "hang out" in Heaven with our loved ones. Or spend all of our time singing praise to God?

Do you think God is so egotistical He would require that? Would you expect your own children to endlessly worship you and forfeit achieving their own potential?

Looking at that from another angle, wouldn't your children indeed be "praising you" through achieving their fullest potential?

If you're beginning to grasp the Collective, the answer should be clear. By re-entering life and experiencing, we praise God eternally. We accomplish this through reincarnation.

We Know Who We Are and Why We Are Here

195

Do I need to believe in reincarnation?

Before we reach the "meat and potatoes" of reincarnation, I want to point out that it's not necessary for you to embrace the belief of reincarnation to achieve abundant living and happiness. My goal with this book is not to establish a belief system for you, but rather to lead you to your truth.

Personal beliefs and happiness are never found "without" – from outside sources – but are always found within.

Within you, God and happiness await.

If you finish this book and can close it feeling more optimistic about life, possessing a greater sense of all things being connected, better able to appreciate "the small things", or at least having unraveled one of life's ubiquitous mysteries, I have succeeded in my endeavor, and you have succeeded in yours.

In my very early days of spiritual exploration, I did not believe in reincarnation. My views mirrored some Christians, feeling that our souls went someplace – I wasn't sure where – until the great arrival of "Judgment Day". And afterwards, following this wondrous "Judgment Day" all souls were doomed to either eternal torture in Hell, or eternal boredom in Heaven, singing praise to God for all eternity.

As the years passed and I began to piece together Life's puzzle, I could never get all the pieces to fit. Every time I would discover some new and exciting "puzzle-piece island" or continent, this new section failed to interlock with the counterparts I had already assembled.

I realized then there was something missing from my puzzle. And despite the persistent signs and guidance from my guardian angels, I refused to believe that missing part was reincarnation.

I simply didn't want to believe in reincarnation because it opened too many possibilities.

Yet later, after the continued urging of my spirit guides and blatant signs I saw in life, I finally – begrudgingly – decided to give reincarnation a look.

It was at that point when my own puzzle went from "flat" to "globe". A light came on, and all the pieces suddenly interlocked, giving structure to chaos and making sense arise from the ash of confusion.

Reincarnation was the "Oceans' of my life puzzle – the common element connecting all of Life's "continents" (the issues we grapple). And through this vast sea, a soul could sail from one "continent" to the next, thus giving the other continents a broader purpose for existing.

How does it work?

As was described in the earlier section on "Death", after we "die", we emerge on "the other side" where we are greeted by friends and family who have crossed and await us.

Immediately afterwards, we are "judged". This "judgment" however, does not occur as Man imagined it, with either the reward of eternal life or the punishment of being "cast into the Lake of Fire" – but rather through a review of your life.

Upon this "judgment", you are approached by a being of light, whose love is warm and overwhelming. Without speaking, this being asks you what good part of your life you can show, and simultaneously, in a panoramic fashion, you see a "review" of your life playing like a big-screen movie.

In this "movie", you see yourself growing from infant to child, from teen to adult, and so on. And although this movie plays at an incredibly fast rate of speed, you are somehow able to absorb every moment and action. You recall each pivotal moment as if it were happening. You understand how each of your decisions affected not only you, but also others in a ripple effect. You see how you learned from certain experiences, and where you overlooked other learning opportunities (such as demonstrated by the parable of The Stove).

You also see how God and Those Watching Over You (your Guardian Angels) created coincidences in life to help you recognize those opportunities and grow spiritually. You see how at other times, they erected "barriers" to deter (but not prevent) you from straying from your elected path. And in either case, whether you were encouraged to follow one path, or deterred from another, the "signs" were provided in a manner that did not thwart your "free will".

In a sense, you realize this "life review" is your "Judgment Day". You see the "Heaven" you brought to "Earth" through unconditional love, and the "Hell" you caused by fear-based actions.

The being of light, however, does not condemn your mistakes. With pure unconditional love, He instead focuses on the good you did, how your actions helped others, and your continuing potential to grow and learn.

After this "life review", you are given time to reflect and communicate with the loved ones who are there. At the same time, you become aware of your previous lives and journeys, and how in each of those, you sometimes "failed" and sometimes triumphed. You become aware of why you plotted your most recent course: the "karma" you wanted to undo, the lessons you hoped to learn.

Upon remembering this – remembering that you are Divine by default – you also become aware of the purposes for your loved ones' journeys. You gain solace knowing that when your loved ones "cross over", you can be there to greet them...

..or you may choose to re-enter life – reincarnate – choosing a "path" and "speed" where your life might "intersect" with loved ones and help them achieve their goals.

Having "free will", the choice to reincarnate is always "souly" yours. It is neither forbidden, nor required.

Sharing the experience of "Life" with your heavenly loved ones, you realize how each and every one of your collective thoughts and actions impacted others on Earth. You realize how collectively, being divine by default, your perceptions of "life" formed the very continents and issues that you (and those near you) had faced.

Upon perceiving this, you understand how – had We (the collective) realized our Divinity while upon Earth – we could have controlled the environment, created "things", and thus lived life more abundantly. In effect, we could have brought "Heaven" to "Earth" and merged the "spiritual" with the "physical". You also see how, over time, we (Mankind) have been progressively unraveling the "cosmic egg" of our purpose. And you see how this "cycle" occurs not only within "Mankind" in general, but also within each and every life form.

Upon realizing this collective goal, you find yourself filled with ambiguity. A part of you wants to stay in Heaven and be with your long-lost loved ones. Another part wants to "check in" on those you've left behind on Earth. And yet another part wants to return to Earth in a physical form, both furthering your own learning and helping the collective.

You realize that, by plotting a different course in "life" and carefully planning the speed, you can "design" your life to experience other "continents" or "classrooms". You can also "time" your life so that you encounter the elements and issues that will help you spiritually advance.

As the enormity of having "eternity" settles in, your ambiguity fades. You realize you are free to help Those on Earth, and can go about plotting and planning you own future visit to return to Earth.

Why do we reincarnate?

As I mentioned earlier, our primary reason for reincarnation is to experience, and thereby help the collective. But there are many other reasons we choose to reincarnate.

Suppose for a moment, that during your "life review", you realized that one of your actions threw another being completely "off their intended track" and thereby prevented them from completing their own life mission.

If you could "go back" in another form, and redirect that person, would you?

Or suppose for a moment, that your own "passing" had left your partner lonely and destitute. And suppose you knew that if you returned as a certain house cat, you would be "owned" by that loved one, providing them with solace.

Would you go back?

If you're thinking: "That's crazy. Who would want to be a cat?" Perhaps you can answer these questions:

Who would want to be a masochist?

Who would want to be a sadist? A wife-beater? A mass murderer? A thief?

Do people not choose to be these things?

If you're having difficulty grasping this subject, let's pretend for a moment that you are a soul who sojourns in heaven in between return trips to Earth. And while in heaven, you are aware that your soul is eternal. You do not have all knowledge, but do possess the knowledge of all your lifetimes – the good and the bad. And as a soul, you are the sum of your experiences. This sum determines Who You Are, and Who You Are adds to the All and Everything.

Now let's suppose that over the last 20 lifetimes, you've returned to Earth as a human. Having said that, knowing you have eternity at hand, is it so hard to believe we might want to return as a simple house cat? Wouldn't some part of a cat's life be appealing? Wouldn't it be nice to be so physically agile and leisurely with life for a few years out of eternity?

Still not convinced you'd ever be a cat?

I'm using "cats" as an example here for a specific reason. Cats are "the preferred physical vehicle" for returning to earth to "observe" life and loved ones. (The ancient Egyptians may have known or believed this... and thus worshiped cats). Using this "vehicle", souls can both experience life, and observe life, at the same time.

If you think about it, after a few of the wearisome lifetimes as a human, coming back as a cat, or dolphin, or penguin, or even a tortoise might not look too bad.

Or how about as a bird, with the ability to fly?

Have you noticed that, since the time of Eden, both plant and animal life on Earth has decreased while human life has increased? And have you noticed that, at any given time there is a long list of "endangered species".

Why do you think that is?

Could it be that more and more souls are spiritually "evolving" and returning to Earth as "human"?

And have you ever noticed how some people have physical or behavior characteristics of animals – often those unrelated to science's "chain of evolution" (ape-to-man)?

Why do you suppose that is?

Could it be they were an "animal" in a recent life?

In James Van Praagh's Talking to Heaven: A medium's message of life after death, he states:

"When an animal comes through during a reading as in the last case, a client usually looks at me somewhat perplexed. We don't think of little Fluffy or Rover surviving death. But why not? Animals are made of the same God-given life force as humans."[15]

Why is it we ascribe our pets with human characteristics, yet we consider them "mere animals"?

How is it that we may describe a dog or a horse as having "soulful eyes", yet we think of them as "soul-less creatures"?

Think about it...

And what about plants?

In The Secret Life of Plants[16] – a book I'd highly recommend – it was shown that plants have a much more involved and encompassing life than we typically attribute to them. Not only do they eat, breath, and move, they also communicate, are aware of their surroundings, grieve at the death of other living organisms, have memories, and can even attune to their caretakers and respond when the caretaker is hundreds of miles away!

Would it be so bad to return as a "lily of the field" and bask in the sun-light while being admired for beauty?

One of Man's challenges is to reconsider his perceptions of animals, plants, and insects. While these "life forms" are different forms of Life, they are all part of the collective.

As humans, the self-appointed "highest" animal, we have certain attributes that are different than those of "lower" animals. For one, we have an opposed thumb which allows us to grasp. For another, we have a mind that enables the power of reasoning. Combining these two, we can build tools and houses and factories and computers and things upon things.

We can create.

Yet we are not "superior" – we are simply "different". Were it not for having these characteristics, Man is very ill-equipped to survive. We do not have the sense of smell of a dog, the speed of a cheetah, the strength of a bull (or horse or bear), the power and agility of a lion... or even the stealth of a lowly mouse.

As with many lessons in the Bible, we have listened but did not learn.

Or better said, we learned in the manner which best suited our ego.

For example, many people are familiar with God giving Man "dominion" over animals as demonstrated by the following scripture:

"And God said, Let us make man in our image, after our likeness, and let them have dominion over the fish of the sea, and over the fowl of the air, and over the cattle, and over all the earth, and over every creeping thing that creepeth upon the Earth".
Genesis 1: 26
The Bible
KJV

In speaking with a Christian minister about this subject, the minister said that Man was indeed "superior" because he was exclusively given "the breath of life" – direct from God – and thereby "became a living soul", as demonstrated in Genesis 2:7:

"And the Lord God formed man of the dust of the ground, and breathed into his nostrils the breath of life; and man became a living soul."
Genesis 2:7
The Bible
KJV

Yet this minister stumbled when I pointed out the reference to "one breath" in the following :

I said in mine heart concerning the estate of the sons of men, that God might manifest them, and that they might see that they themselves are beasts.
For that which befalleth the sons of men befalleth beasts; even one thing befalleth them: as the one dieth, so dieth the other; yea, they all have one breath; so that a man have no preeminence above a beast: for all is vanity.
All go unto one place; all are of the dust, and all turn to dust again.
Ecclesiastes 3: 18-20
The Bible
KJV

He also had difficulty with the following:

O deliver not the soul of thy turtledove unto the multitude of the wicked: forget not the congregation of thy poor for ever.
Psalm 74:19
The Bible
KJV

The problem is, Man has conveniently confused "dominion" with "superiority". Because of his own insecurities, fearing that he might not be God's "favored" creature, Man set out to prove himself right and convince himself he was "above" the animals. He accomplished this through glorifying some scriptures, while ignoring others.

("See... it's written there. That proves it!")

But let's back up for a moment and take a deeper look at the scripture in question:

"And God said, Let us make man in our image, after our likeness, and let them have dominion over the fish of the sea, and over the fowl of the air, and over the cattle, and over all the earth, and over every creeping thing that creepeth upon the Earth".
Genesis 1: 26
The Bible
KJV

In case you hadn't noticed earlier, there's one very interesting element contained in this scripture. Printed in "bold", you will notice the precise use of plural pronouns.

Why do you think that is?

If "Man" had not yet been created, who do you suppose God was talking to? Was He talking to himself? Why use the plural pronouns "us" and especially "our" when He had previously used singular references? In addition, why address "man" as "them" when He was only making "Adam"? And why state in the next verse "male and female he created them" (Genesis 1:27) when he was only creating Adam (and later made Eve from Adam's rib)?"

The reason this occurred was due to the tale of Adam and Eve being symbolic. It was meant to convey a specific lesson of Man's accepting to experience.

The story of Creation is also symbolic and was meant to convey a different message. It was a "preface" of sorts, demonstrating that we can create by believing and speaking (Let there be light – and there was). It also imparted the purpose of creation is "to experience and appreciate" (God "created" then "saw it was good"). It conveyed that all life – plant, insect, aquatic, and animal – were part of the whole, and were also "good". And Man, being created in God's image, was given "dominion" over the "lesser" creatures because of his ability to "create" and shape the world.

Herein, we were given the first and most basic lesson.

Knowing that all things are energy – that our life force is energy – and energy is eternal – you should now know why God used the plural pronouns. The reason is, we were there all along. We were the trees and the roses and the bears and fish and every part of the world that He created. And we wanted to be and experience those things. It was part of our journey to enrich The Tree of Knowledge; part of our spiritual evolution.

The Bible, however, is not the only book to include references to reincarnation. Nor is it the most clear. The Tibetan Book of the Dead[17], which is followed by thousands of monks, provides a very clear and detailed description of "life after life", Karma, and reincarnation.

How we reincarnate:

We each began "life" – that is, experience the physical realm – as a very "simple" life form. Using human terms and definitions to explain this, these are lives that are very short in duration and focus on "survival" in the physical world. They are the "pre-school" and "kindergarten" classes of spiritual advancement, teaching us the ABCs of "existence" in the physical realm. We needed to learn these lessons so that later, we could stay longer and learn larger lessons. We might equate these lives to exploring the tiniest, most barren islands on our Life's Puzzle.

As we "evolve" and learn the ABC's of physical existence, we begin to tackle larger, more complex issues, such as discerning "right" from "wrong". For example, as you look at the animal chain, certain animals (especially our "food" animals) appear oblivious to "right" and "wrong". Whereas other animals (especially predators) – cats, dogs, fox, wolves, lions, bears, (etc.) – appear to comprehend the basics of "right" and "wrong".

As we discussed earlier, the concepts of "right" and "wrong" are both misnomers and cannot exist in the presence of unconditional love. There are, however, certain "actions" and "consequences" that follow universal law. We must learn these "laws" in order to continue our spiritual evolution.

Can we "fail" a grade?

Yes. We can "fail". But again "failure" is an incorrect term. We never "fail" and always learn from every life. Yet at times our "wrongful" actions may cause our life to be "cut short" and thus prevent us from achieving spiritual advancement. Or our life may be ended prematurely due to the actions of others – thus forcing us to "repeat the grade" and creating "karma" for both ourselves and the offender. (We'll discuss Karma later, when looking at the Law of Just Rewards).

Can we repeat a grade?

Yes. Having "free will", we are free to choose any life form we desire. We are never denied reincarnation in any form, and often choose to "repeat a grade" to explore all the lessons that specific "grade level" offers. For example, a student in the fourth grade may end the year with "As" in Science, but "Ds" in History. Having "eternity" to learn, we may choose to "repeat" the grade and focus on better learning "History".

While here in the physical realm, this is all very difficult to imagine because we're so influenced by the aspect of "time". In the spiritual realm however, being able to recall all of our past lives and thoroughly understanding our own goals and that of the collective, our outlook is quite different. With the absence of "time", there is never a need to "rush" or try to skip grades. Like a good meal, each taste of life should be savored.

Choosing our "school":

In addition to choosing our "grade level", we are also free to choose our "school". That is, before entering life, we carefully select the "time" period in which we will live, the country and community where we will reside, our ethnic backgrounds, parents, our likes and dislikes, our skills and challenges, and all the factors helpful in achieving our goal.

What about our "memories"?

As one last point on reincarnation, I need to explain a point mentioned much earlier: how we each individually arrive at the question "What is my purpose in life?"

To answer this, we'll first look at some other mysteries in life that are directly entwined with our soul purpose and reincarnation. We'll begin by looking at our memories.

Have you ever noticed how one memory can cause you to recall another, earlier memory?

Along the same lines, have you ever wondered why people have vivid memories of events from 20, 30, or even 50 years earlier – yet at age 7 we couldn't remember being age 3 (only 4 years earlier)?

The reason for this phenomenon is simple. As souls, when we are in Heaven between reincarnations, we are aware of all of our previous lifetimes and memories.

The problem we face, however, when re-entering "life" is our "memories". We can't "erase" our memories completely, but we need to "repress" them to prevent any "new" memories from triggering earlier ones to resurface. Moreover, we may want some of these repressed memories to surface at a later point in our life, when the timing is appropriate, to serve as directional guideposts.

To achieve our goal, we pass through a spiritually metamorphic state that occurs during what we (as humans) call the "Infancy" and "Toddler" states. During these states, we repress many memories to hide our true identity from ourselves. This repression is performed very selectively so as not to repress memories we learned as simpler life forms (such as how to eat, breath, etc. – lessons we mistakenly term "instincts").

This process of memory repression is why we seldom have memories from infancy and the "toddler" years. It is not that our mind worked so differently that it was incapable of retaining long-term memory, but rather because this memory repression masked those memories.

There is also a much deeper purpose for my pointing out this "memory repression process".

Before our memories were repressed, we were aware that we are Divine in nature. And as if to inadvertently supplicate our knowledge of this, the moment we are born, we have a host of larger, more powerful beings (adults) catering to our every whine and cry.

At some point during our early childhood, however, we give ourselves the biggest "slap-in-the-face" spiritual lesson of all. That is, we allow ourselves to receive "hints" that we are Divine by nature, then take those hints away.

At the undetermined instant this happens, we begin to perceive ourselves as just one of the multitudes. This "revelation" gives birth to the age-old question we all face:

(If I am not special...) "What is my purpose in Life? Why am I here? What is the meaning of Life?"

This "memory repression" system is utilized with all return journeys to earth, regardless of the form we choose. It is also linked to what we refer to as "Deja vu".

The repeat of the cycle:

This process brings us full cycle, emerging us on our latest "continent" of life's puzzle. As we embark on our newest journey, we find ourselves wondering "why are we here?". We sense that we know the answer to this question, yet we cannot recall that answer.

The memory eludes us.

Upon reaching this point, it is akin to a child finding a picture puzzle. Seeing graphics on each piece, the child suspects that when the puzzle is assembled, an insightful picture will be revealed. Yet while looking at individual pieces, the complete picture remains a mystery. And meanwhile, the excitement of life beckons. Everywhere we look, there are enigmas to be explored. A pathway through life awaits us. And while this path is not "predestined", we find it enticing.

Without our knowledge, we have blue-printed our life in a manner that encourages us to encounter certain experiences.

This book is such an example. As I said long ago, it is no coincidence it has reached you or you have found it. Everything in life happens by design, for a specific reason.

In the next section on "Communications", we'll discuss this phenomenon in greater detail.

Answers await the curious.

Chapter 20
Communications from God

Suppose for a moment God decided He would pay a visit to Earth and materialize in human form...

What do you think would happen?

Would all the people of Earth flock to worship Him? Would all the animals? Would all the governments put politics on hold and suddenly unite Worldwide? Would crimes cease to occur? Would trade embargo stop? Would there be sudden Global peace? The end of disease and famine?

Or would there be a third World War?

I pose to you that God's "arrival" on Earth would mark the most devastating event we could ever imagine.

Why?

Think about it. There would be those who would flock to Him and fall upon their knees in reverence. And opposite, there would be those who claim: "That is not the true God! He is the Devil in disguise, here to deceive us! He is the Anti-Christ!" And any miracles He would perform to prove He was God would be discounted as "false miracles" of the anti-Christ.

There would be other factions, too: those who neither believed nor disbelieved, awaiting proof. And those who claimed that God was solely their Deity and not the God of other religions.

And naturally, those who perceived Him as the Anti-Christ would do everything possible to assassinate or destroy him and his followers. While those who proclaimed him God would go to any means to protect Him.

We would indeed be in the midst of Armageddon.

The good news for us is, God is already aware of this. And better yet, He is already with us – and we are with Him. Collectively, all things are God. He need not take on human form to communicate with us, or guide our lives. He can already do this through simpler, more personal means.

COMMUNICATING

There are many ways God communicates with us. He sends intuitions we feel in our hearts, images we see with our mind's eye, coincidences that can direct and guide our lives, and dreams which provide us with insight through a blend of images and feelings. All we need to do is listen.

Let's look at these individually.

INTUITION

> "The only real valuable thing is intuition."
> Albert Einstein[18]

214

What is intuition?

According to my trusty desk copy of the Merriam-Webster Dictionary[19], the working definition of "intuition" is:

"the power or faculty of knowing things without conscious reason".

Referring back to an earlier definition, "knowledge" is defined as:

"understanding gained by actual experience (a ~ of carpentry); something learned and kept in the mind."

As you can see, "intuition" and "knowledge" are very similar in their definition. The fundamental difference between the two are the source of information. "Knowledge" is acquired through experience. It comes by gathering and analyzing information from outside sources. If we learn to cut boards, hammer nails, level doorways, and square walls, we will begin to acquire a basic "knowledge" of carpentry.

"Intuition", however, occurs without watching and learning. It is a form of knowledge that just springs up inside us!

Why?

Because it's either "remembered" by you (by revealing a repressed memory), or planted there by God.

This should be another one of those "no-brainer" moments for you. How else could this information just form inside of us?

So the question is, how does God do this?

He does this using the "Language of the Universe" – emotion.

In all species, human or animal, we can see love and fear, anger and joy, contentment or discomfort, and we can identify – interpret – those emotions. Feelings (emotions) are the language of the Universe.

So why do we not speak using this Universal language all the time?

The answer is simple.

As children, we start out life speaking the Universal language. (Does a baby not cease to cry when cuddled?) But very soon, at a very young and tender age, we learn that others can and will steal our energy. They will dominate us, lie to us, or even hurt us in order to do so.

When this first occurs, the experience forces us to "raise our guard" to protect and preserve our life force. It gives birth to fear and cynicism. We begin to distrust everyone and everything in general.

We want "proof" of everything we hear and see (herein lies the success of modern science). We want our own feelings "validated" before we trust them (the success of psychology), and we want to be told what to believe and what is true before we wholeheartedly embrace it (the success of organized religion).

We often refuse to believe our "instincts" and will opt over them for "logic" because we can't verify the source of these intuitions.

Like any wall, the guard we erect not only keeps out the bad, but also keeps out the good. We inadvertently block energy (in the form of emotions) we would otherwise freely receive. Through our perceptions and fears, we become "individualized" and separate ourselves from the collective. By raising our guard, we are blocked from receiving precious life force, and thus are forced to test and use the four Personality Modes (as described earlier).

Through this entire process, we create an obvious problem. By having erected our guard, we can no longer communicate using the Universal language. Therefore, at an early age, we are forced to learn a "human" language in order to communicate. And while this language may function for us and allow us to maintain our guard, we intuitively sense the language is cumbersome. We often find it frustrating when trying to express what we "feel"; words often do not suffice.

And we are not alone in this problem.

For these same basic reasons, every species on our planet develops its own unique language so it can communicate with those of its kind while protecting its own life force. Like the language of humans, most of these languages consist of sounds, body posturing, and motions. Some are loud and animated (such as the chatter of monkeys) while others are subtle and hard to perceive (such as that of reptiles).

To look at an example that most people may relate to, we can consider dogs. We know that dogs wag their tails when they're happy, and growl when they're angry or threatened. They can also laugh, mew, lick their chops, whine, howl, pant, stand rigid, roll on their back, and even beg when hungry. Put two dogs together, and we can watch them "speak" to each other. This is the language of dogs. We've all likely seen it and can interpret the major expressions.

Cats, horses, rats, mice, and dolphins also exhibit their own unique languages – as do all living things – even plants. To witness it, you only need to take the time to observe.

Having said that, I'm going to make a brief detour from our subject to point out an unmentioned aspect. Every species also exhibits the four major Personality Modes in their own manner.

217

Here again, we can use dogs as an example:

Growl / Bristling – Intimidator
Bark / Cocked ears / Inquisitive Looks – Interrogator
Whine / Beg / Rolling on back – Poor me
Being alone / silent – Aloof

And here again, they use the major PM's for the same reasons we do – getting the attention their life force craves.

As humans, we have developed our own language of words and motions. The language may vary from country to country, but the fundamentals are the same. We can say "I care" to verbalize an expression. We can hug or kiss on the cheek to demonstrate that same expression, or we can do all of these simultaneously to emphasize and supplement the expression.

What we often fail to recognize is, we can send this same message using the Universal language. We each have this ability, and see it in rare glimpses of life.

When we "connect" with another person – that is, when we drop our defenses and guards – we can send the message "we care" without saying or expressing it. If you think back to the parable of the two lovers in the mall, you can see this phenomena at work. The two lovers each "intuitively" sensed the other loved them. Because they felt comfortable with each other, they had dropped their guards and were being open and sharing. And what were they sharing? What caused that "lover's glow"?

Emotion.

And what is emotion?

Energy.

Is it beginning to come clear?

Without realizing it, "Jane" was "eavesdropping" on the two lovers. She intuitively knew the mall couple were lovers because she overheard them telling each other "I love you" in the Universal language.

This is the language of emotion.; the preferred method God uses to "talk" to us. He uses this because emotions are difficult to misinterpret.

By sending us internal feelings – intuition – God can convey what is true or false, what is "right" or "wrong", what is good or bad, likely or unlikely, safe or dangerous – all in a very clear manner. And even though we may not be able to explain exactly what we feel or how we arrived at our conclusion – its origin – we cannot deny "knowing".

Messages from God are never denied us. We need only ask and listen.

> [Christ speaking]"And I will pray the Father, and he shall give you another Comforter (The Holy Spirit – intuition), that he may abide with you for ever; Even the Spirit of Truth; whom the world cannot receive [understand/accept], because it seeth him not, neither knoweth him: but ye know him; for he dwelleth with you, and shall be in you."
>
> St. John 14: 16,17
> The Bible
> KJV

> For ye have not received the spirit of bondage again to fear... the Spirit itself beareth witness to our Spirit that we are the children of God.
>
> Romans 8: 15,16
> The Bible
> KJV

219

"Ask, and it shall be given you; seek, and ye shall find; knock, and it shall be opened unto you. For every one that asketh receiveth; and he that seeketh findeth; and to him that knocketh it shall be opened."

St. Matthew 7: 7,8
The Bible
KJV

MENTAL IMAGES

Mental images work on the same principle as intuition. They are the second cornerstone of the Universal language. Just like our language has both words and gestures, the Universal language has mental images and emotions, respectively.

You might think of it like satellite TV reception. If you have one of the satellite systems that use "AV" lines, you have one line for "video" and a separate line for "sound". The Universal language works on this same principle. With every "video" transmission (mental image) that is sent, there is a simultaneous broadcast of "sound" (feelings).

The problem is, most of the time we're not fully "tuned in", or have our guard up, and can only pick up one or the other of these signals – often intermittently . Beyond that, our "reception" may oscillate between the two, which causes us to receive confusing messages.

Those we call psychics, mediums, or clairvoyants are usually more in tune with one or more of these lines.

To remedy our reception problem, we merely need to connect with God on a more frequent basis. The more we become "in tune" with God, the clearer our reception will become.

COINCIDENCES:

Many years ago, when I was a young "student of the Universe", I debated the matter of coincidences with a friend who happens to be an Episcopal minister. When I asked his opinion about coincidences potentially being "sources of divine guidance" (inspiration, or intervention), he argued that they were not. The basis for his belief was that:

1). God gave Man "Free Will" to make his own decisions and choose his own destiny. (We'll discuss "Free Will" and "Destiny" shortly).

2). Through the process of making these decisions, Man's own actions created the coincidences.

3). Coincidences were just "random occurrences in life".

4). Just like a coincidence might cause a person to step out of the path of a speeding bus, a coincidence could also cause a person to step into the bus's path – and that wasn't a work of God.

All this, he said, served as proof that "coincidences" were merely consequences of Man's "free will" decisions.

Considering this, I posed another question to the minister (we'll call him "Larry" for reference).

"Is God, indeed, all-knowing?"
"Of course," Larry said, "God knows all things."
"Does he know the future?"
"Well, yes. Of course God knows. In the old Testament, through prophets, He foretold the coming of Christ and many events."
"So if a man were about to step in front of a bus, God would

know it?"

"Well, yes. I suppose he would..."

"Then Larry, if God loves us as His children, don't you think God would try to stop it?"

"No. I don't. To do so, God would be interfering with the Free Will he promised Man."

"But didn't God give Man the gift of prophecy, and encourage Man to prophesy?"

"Yes. Among many other gifts: the greatest being Charity or Love."

"So if a man had the gift of prophecy and could foresee that another man was about to step in front of a speeding bus, don't you think the man should use his gift, in a benevolent fashion, to prevent the accident? And if not, what good is the gift? And why should a Man use it to prevent an accident if God would not?"

Larry started to reply, but was at a sudden loss of words.

"Let's consider another angle, Larry. If coincidences are just random consequences of Man's actions, how does God know the future?"

"I'm not sure I follow what you mean by that."

"Let's look at Nostradamus, who supposedly predicted Hitler's rise to power some 500 years before it occurred."

Larry chuckled. "I don't necessarily believe in Nostradamus' abilities."

"That's okay, let's just assume Nostradamus had the gift of prophecy. If what you're saying is true, that coincidences are just "random consequences of Man's actions", then it would have been virtually impossible for Nostradamus to predict the future."

Larry leaned forward. "I'm still not sure I'm following you... but go on."

"If coincidences are random consequences of Man's actions, and have no link to God, then the future is completely uncertain."

"I'm listening."

"In other words, suppose Hitler's parents, or his grandparents, or his great grandparents, or even his great-great grandparents, met due to a coincidence that occurred between the time of Nostradamus' prediction and Hitler's birth. Had someone along the lineage not made a certain choice or decision, there's a strong chance that the coincidence then wouldn't have occurred and Adolph Hitler would have never been born."

Larry scratched his chin.

"Or suppose Hitler himself failed to 'come to power' due to a similar coincidence...or lack thereof...that should have occurred within his lifetime. An event that was created or negated by the choice of another man... or even Hitler himself."

"I see what you're saying. But I don't think it works that way. I think God knows what decisions we'll make before we even make them. Even though this is impossible for Man to know."

"Then you believe in Fate? That all our decisions are pre-determined?"

"No, I believe in Free Will. That Man makes each decision as he encounters each new issue."

"Okay. Let's see if I have this straight. You believe that Man has free will, but God knows our decisions before we make them?"

"Right."

"So in other words, if a man is driving to work tomorrow, and the engine happens to go out of his car right in front of a car dealership, God already knows whether the man will choose to have the engine repaired, or will opt to buy a new car."

"That's right. And if the man is going to buy a new car, God already knows the model, price, and color."

"But if God already knows this is going to occur, doesn't that mean it's predestined?"

"No. It's not predestined, God just knows the decisions this man will make, before he makes them."

"But Larry, if God knows these decisions, then He must also know the repercussions of those decisions, too, right? Otherwise, how could he know that the next issue/decision point would ever be reached... such as buying a replacement car? For example, how could he know that the man doesn't step in front of a speeding bus when climbing out of his car after it breaks down?"

Larry swallowed. "Well, I guess God must know what consequences are going to occur."

"Then couldn't the fact the man's car conveniently broke down in front of the car dealership have been a work of God – a coincidence created by God?"

Larry was at a loss for words.

While there are some people who may believe that coincidences are merely random happenings – consequences of our actions – we need not look far to find the truth. The world around us is a mass of carefully balanced eco-systems and complexities. It is wondrous beyond comprehension. Nature demonstrates this every day.

Is it not amazing that trees and plants breathe carbon dioxide and effuse oxygen while mammals do the exact reverse – thus creating a balance? Is it not amazing that inside our own bodies we have "good" bacteria and "bad" bacteria that hold each other in check while keeping us, and them, healthy? Is the cycle of reproduction not amazing? The cycle of the seasons? The tide?

If you were God (and you are, of course), would you create such a complex world and then just allow coincidences to "run amuck" and disturb or destroy the balance you strived to create?

Of course not.

I believe Albert Einstein summed this up best by saying:

"I cannot believe that God would choose to play dice with the universe."
Albert Einstein[20]

As we've already explored, God is truly and wholly 'all-knowing" ("omniscient" as some prefer to say). He knows when a "sparrow falls from a tree" and knows every action and re-action.

How does He know?

224

Because He is ALL THINGS.

We've been told this many times before, yet have not acknowledged the fundamentals.

In Neale Donald Walsch's book[21], the author attributes God to say:

I tell you this: There is no coincidence, and nothing happens 'by accident.'

"Free Will" vs. Destiny":

Before we can continue exploring the topic of coincidences, let's take a moment to address the age-old clash between "Free Will" and "Destiny". Below, I've provided some loose definitions for our use here.

"Free Will":

The concept of Free Will is based on Man's ability to make each decision as he encounters each issue, therefore allowing Man to choose his own pathway. In other words, nothing in life is "pre-determined". The future is completely unformed, and the ultimate outcome depends on the choices made by Man as he makes the journey.

"Destiny ("Fate")":

The concept of "Destiny" opposes that of "Free Will" by 180 degrees. Those who believe in Destiny, believe that our path in life is already "pre-determined". Our decisions and the hurdles we will face in life are also pre-determined before we even encounter

225

them. "Fate" enables the possibility of "prophecy". The shortfall of believing in Destiny, however, is that many people do not like the concept of feeling our decisions are pre-determined. We want to feel that we are "fully in charge" of plotting our own destiny and not bound to a given "fate".

Reconciling Fate and Destiny:

On the surface, it appears that these two extremes can not be reconciled. However, as you have seen, through reincarnation they are indeed reconcilable. Whenever we re-enter life, we do so with the goal of experiencing certain pleasures and tribulations. Our plans are shared with loved ones on the other side – our Guardian Angels or "Spirit Guides" – who have agreed to help us make our journey to experience the aspects of life we wish to learn. In this manner, "Free Will" and "Fate" are reconciled. Because, before entering life, we choose "circumstances" (our parents, our environment, social standings, etc.) that will launch us in the correct direction to experience whatever is needed for our spiritual growth.

We blueprint our lives.

And by having such a blueprint in place, a certain "fate" is likely, but is not pre-determined. This is because God and our Guardian Angels continually "shepherd our way", using what we call "coincidences" to encourage us to follow one path, or deter us from another.

The beauty of recognizing coincidences as "divine guidance" is that coincidences do not interfere with our Free Will. They come to us as "signs", and may present a new doorway for us to enter (or cause a "wrong" door to slam shut in our face). Whether we then enter the open inviting doorway or knock down the closed door is ultimately our choice.

We are still in control.

Coincidences sometimes arrive like a whisper, being hard to perceive unless one is actively "listening". At other times, they can be delivered as blatantly as a slap in the face. And generally speaking, the more obvious they are, the more suggestive it is we follow the path they indicate.

When we "go with the flow" things often "fall into place". But when we try to "force the issue" or "go against the grain", we often find something that "wasn't meant to be".

Many of us can relate to this form of "intervention" through previous failed relationships. Perhaps in your past, you had a relationship that simply wasn't "meant to be". It may be that you truly loved the person and wanted to be with them, but "circumstances" kept you apart. The harder you tried, the more obstacles that got in the way. Perhaps those obstacles were interfering relatives, jealous friends, physical distances, a shortage of time, social standings, mis-communications, or some other unexplainable hurdle. But regardless of how much you wanted that person, "Fate" held you at bay. And later down the road, in hindsight, after you've removed the rose-colored glasses of love, perhaps you can see how and why that person would have been wrong for you.

On the other side of the spectrum, many of us can relate to having a coincidence occur which helped to either guide our lives or ease a decision. Maybe you were driving down the road, pondering a particular issue, and looked up only to find the answer splayed across the face of a billboard. Or perhaps the answer came through the words of a song, a phone call from a friend, a personalized license plate, or some other source we couldn't possibly expect.

And even if you can't recall a specific instance from your own life, many of us have seen stories of this phenomenon on TV shows that investigate (or recount) "miracles". We see tales of two long-lost relatives who are re-united when they end up seated next to

227

each other on the same flight, and happen to strike up a conversation. The story of a man who avoided being struck by a stray bullet when he bent over to pick up a penny off the street. The love story of a couple who met after they both happened to miss their buses and were stranded together at the bus station. Or the woman who loses her keys and can't get in her own house, only to later learn an intruder was waiting inside.

These are all examples of the countless ways God and our Guardian Angels keep us safe and on our intended path of life.

The Fourth Law of the Universe is this:

ALL things happen for a reason. There are no "coincidences" in God's divine plan.

Be it good or bad, significant or trivial, all "chance occurrences" happen for a reason.

The key to experiencing this phenomenon is awareness. Once you become aware that God will guide you through coincidences, all you have to do is wait and watch for coincidences to occur. It's that easy – and you can start the process today.

Right now.

By mentally acknowledging that you will watch for coincidences, you have actuated the process. As you go through the next few days of your life, merely watch for any significant coincidences that occur and follow whatever guidance they suggest.

What constitutes "significant"?

"Significant" coincidences, or as Carl Jung called them – "meaningful"[22] – are occurrences which have the ability to impact your life (or that of another person) OR serve as a method of solving a problem or task at hand.

For example, suppose that you go to a local job fair in hopes of finding a job as a computer technician. While there, in the cafeteria you bump into an old long-lost friend. That, in itself, would be a coincidence but not necessarily a "significant" one. However, as you strike up a conversation with the old friend and catch up on missed time, you learn that they are hosting one of the booths. And it just happens they're trying to recruit a fresh computer technician for their company, and the job opening they have is exactly what you were hoping to find.

Your "coincidence" has now become "significant" because it can impact your life. In addition, it is significant to the long-lost friend because, from their point-of-view, they "bumped into you" and could resolve their own problem through the (same) coincidence.

The impact on your life need not be significant, however, for a significant coincidence to occur.

How is that?

Suppose you decide to visit a relative, but as you climb into your car and prepare to leave, you realize the car's gas gauge shows near empty. And suppose that upon checking your wallet, you see that if you purchase gas, you will only have $10.00 remaining. Knowing you will need this $10.00 to pay for the kid's school lunches, some would assume that "fate" has played a hand and the journey was not "meant to be".

Now suppose that you pray to God, "thanking" (not asking) God for giving you a sign. And suppose that as you climb out of the car, you notice a $10.00 bill lying on the ground. While the trip to visit the relative may not have been significant, the coincidence is very significant due to God's providing this "sign".

As I mentioned earlier, the key to utilizing the guidance of coincidences is awareness. All you need to do is open yourself and stay alert to the signs.

DREAMS

Dreams are another way God and our Guardian Angels communicates with us. If you experience a bizarre dream, with unusual colors, it may result from the 3 slices of pizza you ate just before bedtime. But if you have a clear dream, especially one that repeats itself, you're getting a message. This is especially true if the scenery of the dream changes, but the "theme" remains the same. When this occurs, you're being presented the same message in a different context because you didn't "get it" the first or second time.

I experienced a combination of coincidence and insightful dream after writing the previous section of this book. As I went to bed that night, I thanked God and my Angels to provide any insight that might guide my life. (We'll discuss how to receive insightful dreams shortly).

At some point near dawn, I awoke, recalling a vivid dream. It went as follows:

I "awoke" into the dream, and found myself standing on a platform that was approximately 4' x 4' in size, and was magically suspended in mid air. Like a magic carpet, the platform was hovering above a small, peaceful lake, set in the foothills of dream netherlands.

As I looked down at the platform, I noticed a book laying on one corner. Picking it up, I thumbed through the pages and found that only the first one-half of the book contained any print. The second half was entirely blank.

A sound from below caught my attention and the book mysteriously vanished from my hands. Looking down at the water, I saw several small children and infants – children ranging from the ages of 1 to 8 – children who appeared too young to swim unattended – splashing, laughing, and swimming their way across the lake.

Paddling alongside and amid the children were a mixture of animals. Next to one boy, I saw a small black dog. Beside another child swam a cat. And off to the side swam geese, a pony, ducks, and several other animals.

With a mixture of disbelief and wonder, I watched the mixed group swimming below.

Still amazed by the sight, I looked toward the beach, expecting to see the children's parents also caught in awe. But instead, the parents were mingling among themselves, oblivious to the swimming children and animals.

My awe turned to horror when I spotted a gray silhouette, that of a shark about 10 feet in length – a shark mysteriously swimming in freshwater – gliding silently beneath the surface, headed directly toward the children and animals.

Jumping up and down on the platform, frantically waving my arms, I yelled to the children, trying to warn them to swim to shore. Yet to my dismay, the children couldn't hear me over their own ruckus. I then turned toward the shore, hoping to alert the parents of the children, but found that the shoreline was mysteriously receding away from me, moving into the distance – as if the lake were expanding.

Below, the shark reached the group and began circling beneath them: its head jerking back and forth with agitation.

With no help in sight, I crouched on the edge of the platform and waited for the shark to swim directly beneath me. When it did, I jumped feet-first – my arms and hands flat at my sides – using my body as an air-to-sea missile to actually strike the shark. I knew the impact won't kill the shark. It wouldn't even injure it. The most I could hope was to startle the shark and scare it away long enough for me to herd the children and animals to safety.

Just as I leaped from the platform and plummeted toward the water, I awoke.

The following morning, I had several errands to run, and as I went about them I tried to analyze the dream.

What did it mean? And what message did it carry?

I could sense the dream had meaning and significance, yet the message continued to elude me. The more I thought about the dream, the foggier the details became.

By mid-afternoon, being no closer to an answer, I sat down and played a little word-association game, hoping to unlock the enigma. Thinking of the key elements of the dream, I wrote them down:

Incomplete Book
Platform
Swimming children and animals
Parents
A receding beach
Shark

In the flow of writing, I started jotting down my "personal" definitions of each of these elements. When I reached "shark", I wrote:

Shark – A predator; fish; an unseen threat; hidden danger; surprise attack; stealthy.

Looking back at my list, the dream suddenly became embarrassingly clear to me.

The "incomplete book" represented this book, as I was in the middle of writing it, and it was a foremost issue on my mind. Obviously, the second half of the book was "blank pages".

The "platform" is just that, a platform from which I can present a message.

The message I was being given through the dream, was this:

In an early section, I had discussed energy theft and the four major Personality Modes. I then extended this to show how children develop these PM's. Later, in a recent segment, I showed how animals exhibit the behavior attributed to the four PM's.

What I failed to do, however, was explain that – just like adults – both children and animals are also susceptible to energy theft from would-be predators: "sharks" (which also happens to be an example I used while discussing the "Life of the Party" PM). In other words, I had failed to alert readers (the parents on the beach) of this danger. And until I did so, they were without knowledge of the threat. Moreover, the receding beach signaled that my opportunity to warn the parents was "fading into the distance".

With that said, I have conveyed this message. As adults, it is easy to intimidate children (or animals) and force them to "pay attention". Both emotional and physical abuse are forms of energy theft in this context. As parents or pet owners, we should be aware of this and watch for the "sharks" who pose this hidden danger.

Before we move on to our next topic, I'd like to elucidate one other important aspect of this dream: the timing in which it was delivered. As you can gather from the flow of this text, the dream came at the most appropriate time possible. Had I experienced this dream six months from now, it would have been too late to include its message in publication. Had it come six months earlier – or even a month earlier – it wouldn't have made any sense to me, because I couldn't have foreseen my own forgetting to include things I had not yet written.

Moreover, the fact that I jumped from the platform just before awakening indicated I would find an answer and take action. I'm guessing that whether or not the answer is effective is now up to you, since I "awoke" before seeing the result.

This is the beauty and glory of God's workings. We need only be aware and watchful to see it in action, and use it in our lives.

Chapter 21
Encouraging Communication

As mentioned earlier, not all the communications we receive come directly from God. Some of these messages are relayed to us by "couriers" or those working on our behalf on "the other side".

Each of us have guardian angels (or spirit guides) who constantly watch over us. They guide our lives, and are waiting to meet us when we "cross over". In some cases, our guardians are "specialists" who have already mapped the "continent" we will be traveling. At other times, our guardian angels are friends or relatives who have already "crossed over" and do not yet wish to return to Earth. Whether we know them from this life or one before, they are working in our best interest. Their goal is to help us experience the part of life that we wanted to learn. And in return, the next visit to Earth, we may switch roles with them and watch over them as they cross over. Or we may choose to join them and be watched over by others.

The choice is ultimately ours, and is born of love.

Contacting and communicating with our guardian is very easy and enjoyable. The simplest method is to merely "ask" for their guidance. As a general practice, you may want to develop a habit of including your guardian angels in your prayers. And again, this prayer should be one of thanks, not supplication. It can be as simple as:

"I give thanks to God and my Guardian Angel for watching over me, my family, my pets, and my belongings. Thank you for keeping us safe and for the guidance you constantly provide."

If you want inspiring dreams, you can "ask" for these by including a statement such as:

"And thank you for the clear and insightful dreams you provide me."

or

"Thank you for the coincidences you use to guide my life"

or

"Thank you for the intuitions you provide me".

The list goes on...

If you'd prefer a more "interactive" means of communicating with your Guardian Angel, there is one certain to amaze you.

You may recall that when we discussed setting up the space where you would meet with God, I suggested you have access to electricity and a radio. The reason for this is simple. You can easily communicate with your Guardian Angel through any radio. The steps are easy, and the results are often so astounding they'll prickle the small hairs on your neck and raise goose-flesh on your skin.

Try it and see for yourself:

1. Go to your communion space, where you won't be disturbed, and tune the radio to your favorite station, keeping the volume low and soothing.
2. Think of an issue that's bothering you, vocally or mentally explain this issue, and ask your Guardian Angel to provide you with a *clear* answer on the *3rd full song*. In other words, if there's a song currently playing, it won't count. Jingles in commercials don't count. You're looking for a message in the 3rd full song. You need your question to be clear so your Guardian Angel understands and can provide accordingly.

Why the "3rd" song? Again, 3 is the Universal Number of Harmony (we'll discuss this in the next section). And choosing the 3rd song gives your Guardian time to prepare.

3. As you relax and wait for the 3rd song, think about the issue.

The first time I tried this "interactive" communication, I wanted to get to know my Guardian Angel before relying on answers from a system I hadn't previously tried. The question I asked was:

"What is my Guardian Angel's name?"

Not knowing whether or not this would work, I was chilled when the third song played and I heard Barry Manilow crooning:

> *"Spirit move me, every time I'm near you,*
> *Whirling like a cyclone in my mind.*
> *Sweet Melissa, angel of my lifetime*
> *Answer to all answers I can find."*[23]

237

Have fun with this system of communication. It works, and can work for you.

There are only two basic rules to follow:

1. Never try to use it while driving. My own Guardian Angel has conveyed (emphatically) that they have enough "watching over you" to do while driving, and will ignore petty questions such as "Does so-and-so like me?" rather than put your life at risk (and thus potentially prevent you from achieving your life mission).

2. Never try to abuse or shortcut the system, as in saying "I want an answer for 'this' in the third song, and for 'this' in song 4, and 'this' for song 5," (and so on). You must separate each question with 3 full songs.

Chapter 22
The Fifth Universal Law

The Fifth Law of the Universe is this:

All things that harmonize with the Universe can be measured in denominations of three.

Any item or occurrence that conforms with the Universe can be described, measured, or gauged by 3 details or components.

All of our "cosmic eggs" are paragon examples of this law at work.

The Holy Trinity is a fitting example, and follows the pattern of a "cosmic egg". In this, the "Holy Trinity" consists of Father (1), Son (2), and Holy Ghost (3): one existence with 3 unique facets.

As a closer-to-home example, when speaking in the first person, you would refer to yourself as: "Me, Myself, or I".

When referring to others you use: "he, him, himself" or "she, her, herself", or "they, them, themselves".

We measure distance through: here, there, and the space in between.

Time is measured through:
1. Past, present, future.
2. Then, now, later.
3. Seconds, minutes, hours.

The mind is composed of: conscious, sub-conscious, super-conscious.

A "life form" is composed of: mind, body, spirit.

If you're exceptionally perceptive, you may have detected a parallel between the components of a "life form", and those of the Holy Trinity.

In example:

The Mind is unseen and is the sum of our knowledge; *God* is unseen and is the sum of all knowledge.

The Body is our physical form and is governed by our mind; *Jesus* (the Son) was God in physical form, and performed "the will" of "The Father".

The Soul is our spirit and *life force*; the essence of us that is divine and eternal, allowing us to transcend death and reach the ethereal realm. The *Holy Ghost* is the divinity and *life force* of God. It is the "spirit" of God's divineness and unconditional love.

*Then Peter said unto them, Repent, and be baptized every one of you in the name of Jesus Christ for the remission of sins, and ye shall receive the gift of the **Holy Ghost**.*
Acts 2:38
The Bible
KJV

*If ye then, being evil, know how to give good gifts unto your children: how much more shall [your] heavenly Father give the **Holy Spirit** to them that ask him?*
Luke 11:13
The Bible
KJV

*While Peter yet spake these words, the **Holy Ghost** fell on all them which heard the word.*
Acts 10:22
The Bible
KJV

*And the angel answered and said unto her[Mary], The **Holy Ghost** shall come upon thee, and the power of the Highest shall overshadow thee: therefore also that holy thing which shall be born of thee shall be called the Son of God.*
Luke 1:35
The Bible
KJV

Being divine by nature, the process of Creation also conforms with the Universe and can be compared to the Holy Trinity.

1. Thoughts (the "tools"); God
2. Matter (physical energy); Christ
3. Belief (the driving force); The Holy Ghost

If you want to build a mound, you need (1) a shovel (the tool), (2) effort to move the shovel (the driving force), and (3) dirt (the matter to be rearranged).

When speaking about triads in *Conversations with God, An Uncommon Dialogue*, the author uses many of these same examples. He then shows God discussing "dyads" (groups of two) by saying:

"In matters of gross relationships, you [Mankind] recognize no "in-between". That is because gross relationships are always dyads, whereas the relationships of the higher realm are invariably triads. Hence, there is left-right, up-down, big-small, fast-slow, hot-cold, and the greatest dyad ever created: male-female."[24]

I've included mentioning the Universal law of triads because it serves as a very helpful tool for everyday life. As you go about life and encounter various issues, you can test the validity of each issue by determining if the issue conforms to the "cosmic egg" principle: three separate parts making up a whole.

Being divine by default, we often perform this "divine testing" without realizing we are doing it. For example, if your boss calls you into his office and tells you he's giving you a pay raise and a new title, most people would want to know: *Why – what's the catch?* In this particular instance, we might perceive that we have been told "the positive" (the pay raise) and "the neutral" (the new title). Yet without realizing the underlying mechanics, we suspect a "third" aspect is missing. We feel *"there's something I'm not being told"* and await the bomb to drop. We don't know why or how, but we suspect "something is missing".

This occurs because, subliminally, we know that things "come in threes". And on some subconscious level, we realize we have been told "two" of the "three" necessary parameters – and the third is still missing.

In this example, the missing component might be the "negative" – added responsibilities, longer hours, or higher expectations. It might be any one of these "negatives" alone, or could be a *collective group of negatives* (such as the three in the previous sentence).

I should mention here that polarities (positive and negative) cannot correctly be applied to "Cosmic eggs" in a uniform sense. This is because *polarities are determined by one's perspective.*

For example, to a person who already feels overworked, the aspect of "added responsibilities" might be a heavy "negative". Yet to a worker who is bored with their job, any "added responsibilities" might be perceived as "new challenges", and as a positive.

Just like beauty, "polarity" is determined by the beholder.

Taking that one step farther, a Christian would likely consider the "Holy Trinity" as three "positives". An agnostic might view the Trinity as three "neutrals". An atheist might perceive it as three "negatives".

If you're reading between the lines here, there is a deeper, more insightful lesson at play. As I've mentioned before (and will mention again) – all aspects of life are woven together. At this juncture of our journey, one can see a correlation between "polarity" and "truth". What is the "truth" and absolute for one person, may not be the truth for another.

For the man who sits in prison, *true* freedom may be viewed as being able to move about; to own a car. To have a home. To have a job.

To the working man, these same freedoms may be perceived as his prisons. Therein, the truth for one man is not the truth for another.

As Mr. Einstein showed us, all things are relative. And in this, all three components of any cosmic egg are "neutral" until they are "judged" by the beholder and are applied to the "truth" of his or her relative plane. The polarity we perceive depends on whether our view is based in "love" (positive), "fear" (negative), or indifference (neutral).

Truth can be found in any polarity. However, "Truth" found in *fear* is the equivalent of a prospector finding fool's gold. While he or she may think they have a find of great value, sooner or later they will learn their presumed treasure has little worth at all.

The highest of Truth is found through unconditional love.

So how do we find this Truth?

By beginning on a "neutral" plane, viewing objectively, and then appreciating *all* aspects we encounter during any experience – both the positive and the negative. In doing so, we act with unconditional love. We "accept" the gift of the Holy Ghost.

Chapter 23
The Greatest Deception of All

"I cannot imagine a God who rewards and punishes the objects of his creation, whose purposes are modeled after our own – a God, in short, who is but a reflection of human frailty."
Albert Einstein [25]

Okay. A new subject.

(Or is it new? – All of life is interconnected. All aspects of life occur in cycles).

Suppose that *your* child was being stalked by a child molester.

What would you do?

And suppose you *knew* this molester meant your child harm and was intent on luring the child away with candy. If it was within your power to stop this molester, would you stop them, or would you simply "stand aside" and allow this evil person to potentially succeed?

Before you answer – and the answer should come easily enough – let's take this scenario one step further.

Suppose this molester did indeed successfully lure your child away. And after succeeding, this villain threw your child into a holding cell where he endlessly tortured and tormented them – never killing, yet never allowing the child a single moment of reprieve. And suppose you *knew* the precise location of this holding cell, and could *hear* your child beg for help and could even see their agony.

Would you save them?

I think I'm safe in saying, for most of us – those who are sane – the answer here is clear. To allow one's child to be lured away by some malevolent, evil person would be unthinkable. We'd have to be crazy – demented – certainly an unfit parent – to allow such a horrific event to occur.

And what would we be if we *knowingly* permitted this "evil being" to succeed? What if we passively stood by, ignoring the child's cries of pain and pleas for rescue?

A monster?

Something worse than a monster?

As ludicrous as it seems, the followers of certain religions attribute this "monstrous" behavior to God. It is a veritable cornerstone of their belief system; the premise of "Satan" and "Hell".

In case you're not familiar with the story, allow me to provide a very loose summary.

Supposedly, at some unknown point, God created the angels. And after being created, one of these angels – Lucifer (Satan, Legion, he has many names) – grew discontent and aspired to overthrow God. In an attempt to create a "supernal mutiny", Satan "sinned" (while in Heaven, no less), gathered several other discontent angels into his following, and launched a war against God and the "good" angels.

God, of course, prevailed, and cast Lucifer and his "legion" out of Heaven. And in his anguish, Satan vowed to tempt Man – God's "most prized" creation (see any symmetry here?) – to lure

Man from God.

According to this myth, because God has given Man "free will" to choose his deity, God passively allows Satan to tempt His children (Man) with "candy" (sin) in an attempt to lure Man from God's grace. And upon "Judgment Day", God will judge Man one-by-one, determining who has been faithful, and who deserves everlasting torture in "Hell" (or to be destroyed in the Lake of Fire– depending upon the denomination) .

As you can see, this belief is driven by fear, not unconditional love. It uses the fear of eternal damnation as a tool to insure obedience.

Yet are we not made in God's image? And if we are, considering we (those of us who are sane) couldn't dish out this punishment to our children, why ascribe such cruel and uncaring characteristics to God?

Is it feasible to believe that God might judge His own creation, and would not only allow Satan to "win", but would knowingly damn His creation to "Hell" – to a place where we might suffer for all eternity with *no* chance of reprieve, regardless of how well we "learned our lesson" and beg for forgiveness?

And as you answer – and again the answer should come quickly – bear in mind that God, being *All-knowing,* would be *continually aware* of the suffering and lamentations of these "damned" souls... for all eternity.

Wouldn't this be a form of Hell for a God who loves His children?

Climbing one more step, if God is omnipresent, does that mean He'll be in Hell, too?

In *Conversations With God*, when the author presents the question "What is Hell?", God is cited as saying:

247

There is hell, but it is not what you think, and you do not experience it for the reasons you have been given.
What is hell?
It is the experience of the worst possible outcome for your choices, decisions, and creations. It is the natural consequence of any thought which denies Me, or says no to Who You Are in relationship to Me.
It is the pain you suffer through wrong thinking. Yet even the term "wrong thinking" is a misnomer, because there is no such thing as that which is wrong.
Hell is the opposite of joy. It is unfulfillment. It is knowing Who and What You Are, and failing to experience that. It is being less. That is hell, and there is none greater for your soul.
But Hell does not exist as this place you have fantasized, where you burn in some everlasting fire, or exist in some state of everlasting torment. What purpose could I have in that?
Even if I did hold the extraordinarily unGodly thought that you did not "deserve" heaven, why would I have a need to seek some kind of revenge, or punishment, for your failing?
Wouldn't it be a simple matter for Me just to dispose of you? What vengeful part of Me would require that I subject you to eternal suffering of a type and at a level beyond description?
If you answer, the need for justice, would not a simple denial of communion with Me in heaven serve the ends of justice?[26]

I tell you now that "Hell" does not exist as a physical place. "Hell" is a state of mind. It could be better defined as:

The regrets we suffer due to certain decisions or actions – the memories we bear for eternity.

"Satan" does not exist as a "being". It could be better defined as:

The worldly enticements that prevent us from spiritually advancing.

In effect, "Satan" is "fear". Satan represents the "false Gods" we worship. The "idol" that prevents us from completing our self-assigned life journey; the "sin" we are lured into.

We can see the symbolism in verse:

> *"There is no fear [Satan] in love: but rather perfect love [God] casteth out fear: because fear hath torment. He that feareth is not made perfect in love."*
> *1 John 4:18*
> *The Bible*
> *KJV*

"Satan" [fear] aspired to be "God" [love]: But God [perfect love] cast Satan out of Heaven, because Satan [fear] hath torment [Hell].

By engaging in "sin" – that is, getting caught up in fears of pride, lust, greed, gluttony, etc. – we thwart ourselves from learning and advancing as spiritual beings. We become so mesmerized by one type of experience, we ignore experiencing the other aspects of life that would help us "praise God". And through this, we create our own hell.

Chapter 24
The Law of Just Rewards

Okay. Time for a new subject.

(Or is it?)

The Sixth Law of the Universe is this:

"The Law of Just Rewards".

Most simply put, one might summarize this law by using the old adage:

"What comes around, goes around." (Or vice-versa).

As another rendition, *"every dog has its day"*.

In the Christian context, it is the basis for **"Do unto others as you'd have done unto you."** In Wiccan beliefs, it is sometimes viewed as "Harm none" or "The Rule of Threefold Return". Others might simply say: "You reap what you sow."

Some spiritualists might call this "karma", believing that every action we make is "judged" – deemed good or bad – and that The

Universe keeps a running tab on one's life, suitably punishing (or rewarding) in this life or the next.

As contradictory as it may sound on the surface, I do not believe in karma.

How is that?

Because of a very subtle difference between the common perception of karma, and the Law of Just Rewards.

The Law of Just Rewards has a total absence of "judgment", thus harmonizing it with all other universal laws. As an example we can relate to, we need only look at the "Law of Gravity". If we step off the roof of a two-story building without wearing some type of restraint, we will fall. If we hit the ground and break a leg due to "defying" the Law of Gravity, the broken leg isn't a "punishment". Instead, it is one (of many) predictable consequences to our action.

God – "The Universe" – never "judges" and then dishes out punishments or rewards. Because of truly unconditional love, *there is no right or wrong*. Instead, there are only actions and potential reactions.

But let's look at one more example as further reference.

If a spouse is abusive in a relationship, those who believe in karma might believe this "abuser" would earn "bad karma" against their soul for the wrong-doing. As an end result, during the abuser's current life (or during a following life), they would be "punished" for their "wrong-doing". Their only chance for escaping the bad karma might be through making suitable atonement to the victim.

Yet now that you understand the wider picture, suppose the "victim" in this situation is a "Poor Me", who allows (or even unconsciously encourages) the abuse as a tool to gain life force?

Is this a "debt" the "abuser" must pay for his or her "wrong-doing"? And if so, who deliberates each case and decides?

God?

The answers here are clear. Being *all things*, and having unconditional love for all of His children, God does not judge and issue punishment.

While the pun may be intended, "For God's Sake" He would be judging and condemning *a part of Himself.*

Would God make "Forrest Gump" as "Forrest-Gump-is" and then later condemn him for being "Forrest Gump"?

God loves us unconditionally. And through unconditional love, there is *only* acceptance. Nothing is "right" or "wrong". Instead, there are *only* actions and consequences.

Referring again to Mr. Walsch's book, the author ascribes God as saying:

Consequences are results. Natural outcomes. These are not at all the same as retributions, or punishments. Outcomes are simply that. They are what results from the natural application of natural laws. They are that which occurs, quite predictably, as a consequence of what has occurred.
All physical life functions in accordance with natural laws. Once you remember these laws, and apply them, you have mastered life at the physical level.
What seems like punishment to you – or what you would call

evil, or bad luck – is nothing more than a natural law asserting itself.[27]

"The Law of Just Rewards" is not a form of punishment. It is simply a universal mechanism that allows us to fully experience all extremes. We might relate it to a great pendulum, swinging to-and-fro to guarantee balance within our lives.

In order to appreciate beauty, we must see the ugly. And in order to know joy, we must also know pain. To fully admire "good", we must experience "evil".

To every thing there is a season, and a time to every purpose under heaven:
A time to be born, and a time to die; a time to plant, and a time to pluck up that which is planted;
A time to kill, and a time to heal; a time to break down, and a time to build up;
A time to weep, and a time to laugh; a time to mourn and a time to dance.
Ecclesiastes 3: 1-4
The Bible

On the path of spiritual evolution, as spiritual beings we *want* this balance because it is the only way we can evolve. We can not grow without experiencing both extremes.

So how does the Law of Just Rewards work?

Referring back to "The Delivery System" of the Divinity process, you may recall how the Universe delivers items into one's life through *natural channels*. Each Universal Law works in this same consistent manner. The Law of Just Rewards is no exception. For example, in the case of spousal abuse, a neighbor may overhear a domestic fight and phone the police to report the disturbance, potentially resulting in an arrest and/or criminal charges against the abuser. (As you can see, the neighbor's action could be prompted through *coincidence;* they step outside to carry their trash to the curb and hear the disturbance, etc.).

If the abuser has learned their lesson, realizes the impact of their abuse, and are truly sorrowful for their actions, they can choose to live by what they have learned and end the cycle. If they have not learned the lesson, however, the cycle will repeat; often escalating in intensity.

The more we send out; the more that comes back to us.

For these "slow learners", the Law of Just Rewards progressively becomes more persuasive until the "student" learns *whatever* lesson they have decided to learn. For example, after battering a wife several times, an abusive husband may end up in prison (where he may be abused, and therefore may realize the pain and anguish his actions caused).

In the former paragraph, I italicized the word "whatever" as a prelude to our next point. Most episodes of abuse are not driven by the need to learn "how it feels to abuse", or "how it feels to be abused" – we learned these two lessons long ago, and certainly relearned them during childhood. As we discussed earlier, abuse is often a tool used to steal life force. Corollary to that, the real lesson we may want to learn is how to transcend the Intimidator (or Poor Me) Personality Modes.

If your mind is racing ahead of the text here, you may already be pulling some things together. As we know, people who are abusive are often treated for "anger management".

That is, they are taught that their "anger" and "rage" are based on certain *fears* (often formed during childhood). In order to control the anger, they must uncover the underlying fear, learning to identify, understand, and even *appreciate* the fear for what it is.

(Sound familiar?)

On the opposite side of the abusive relationship, the party being abused may be trying to learn a similar lesson *through a different presentation*. Poor Mes who find themselves in one abusive relationship, often escape that relationship only to wind up later with another abusive partner. They find themselves inexplicably "drawn" or "attracted" to abusive partners, without understanding the hows and whys.

The challenge for a Poor Me is to learn to identify their own reliance on fear by way of being "helpless", "needy" or eliciting "pity". Once they recognize this reliance and become more assertive (such as the Interrogator) or independent (Aloof), they transcend the "Poor Me" cycle.

Before we return to the core of our subject, it's important to point out that Intimidators and Poor Me's are not the only PMs facing challenges in their relationships. Interrogators and Aloofs also face their own relationship challenges, most often in the form of "co-dependency". As we ascend the spiritual ladder, we must first learn not to rely on "fear" to gain our life force (learned as Intimidators and Poor Mes). After we have learned that lesson in several contexts, we must then learn not to rely on "other individuals" or "ourselves" alone (learned as Interrogators and Aloofs). We then ascend to the "Life of the Party" PM, and learn not to depend on "groups" or "intermittent" sources of life force (as a footnote, "Life of the Party" PMs are often challenged with Bi-polar disorders).

After learning these lessons, we finally – sometimes even begrudgingly – turn to spiritual sources: "the collective"; God; the Universe.

By understanding the process, you can choose to "skip grades" and advance directly to The Spiritual mode. The choice is ultimately yours, and there are spiritual "pros and cons" in doing so.

What we must understand is that not all souls operate on the same plateau of understanding. There are those "ahead" and those "behind". Yet this does not make us "superior" to those behind us – no more than we are "inferior" to those ahead. We are all Divine by default and were created equally. Our challenge is to appreciate whatever lesson we are facing.

How does the Law of Just Rewards work when the situation is not "one on one"?

I apologize for that brief digression into PMs but felt that information might be helpful in rounding your overall understanding.

Returning to our core subject, the Law of Just Rewards isn't limited to "abuse" or "one-on-one" situations. As you can probably imagine, it has a myriad of diverse applications. Any type of "wrong" or "right" is subject to The Law of Just Rewards.

As a general rule:

- Negative actions beget negative responses.
- Positive actions beget positive responses.
- Neutral actions beget neutral responses.

Give, and it shall be given unto you; good measure, pressed down, and shaken together, and running over, shall men give unto your bosom. For with the same measure that ye mete withal, it shall be measured to you again.

St. Luke 6: 38
The Bible
KJV

Are you getting it?

If you steal, you'll have something stolen from you. If you abuse, you'll be abused. If you mislead or deceive, you'll be misled or deceived.

If you give, you will receive. If you pay a compliment, you will be complimented. If you love, you will be loved.

God – The Universe – will manifest the "reactions" through natural occurrences or coincidences. The cycle will continue until you learn whatever lesson you must learn.

This is the Law of Just Rewards.

So how does The Law of Just Rewards bridge from one life to the next?

All aspects of life are interrelated, contiguous, and a part of a larger cycle.

To begin exploring this, we might look at the human brain and relate one of its well-known mysteries to some of the things we learned in earlier lessons.

258

It's commonly said that humans only use about 10% of the brain. You may recall that earlier, we discussed how – if a parent or relative in a distant state decides to phone us – part of our subconscious deciphers and "reads" this incoming stream of life force and alerts our conscious mind of this phenomenon. Thus, the "11th" percent of our brain may be a hidden "deciphering" tool for reading life force. The "12th" percent may be the part of our brain used to "send" the transmission.

Another (larger) portion of our "untapped" brain serves as storage space *for memories we don't even realize we have.* You can likely relate to this when an old song plays on the radio, and even though you had long forgotten the song, you find yourself able to sing along, remembering both the melody and words.

Psychologists who work in past life hypnotherapy or regressive hypnotherapy are already aware of our repressed memories. They know that, not only can we remember events from *this life*, we can often recall songs/events/words/names *from our previous lifetimes.*

In the book *You Have Been Here Before* [28], author Edith Fiore shares several fascinating and adventurous recounts experienced during one-on-one regressive-hypnotherapy sessions. These demonstrate the "carry-over" of problems from one life to the next.

In one such recount, a man who suffered from obesity in his current life described earlier lives in which he had died of starvation.

In another setting, a woman who suffered from a fear of sex was able to overcome her sexual inhibitions after being hypnotized, remembering she had been sexually abused in several former lives, and bravely facing that fear.

In another chronicle, a man who was admittedly indecisive in his life, found that he died in previous lives due to repressing his own will in order to please others.

If you're reading between the lines here, you should be able to see a common pattern beginning to emerge tying this to our subject-at-hand. The disorders and phobias that inexplicably plague us in our current lives are actually very rational fears. These fears may stem from our experiences in previous lives. They reside in memories we do not realize we have; memories we ourselves repressed after reincarnation. Memories, we may or may not choose to reveal to ourselves.

Moreover, these past experiences and The Law of Just Rewards are intricately connected. If "Satan" lures us into the sin of "gluttony" for food in one life, and we die from obesity before we complete our life mission, we may be compelled to "repeat that spiritual grade". Because of this, during the following life, we may have an "irrational fear" which typically propels us to the *opposite extreme* of the issue – we so fear becoming obese that we suffer anorexia or bulimia.

Again, recovery comes only when we identify and appreciate – depolarize – the underlying fear.

Our challenge is to *appreciate* all experiences for what they are. By appreciating – by trying to perceive all experiences with a positive mindset – we "let go" of our fear and receive "positive" experiences in return.

In Closing

In closing, I wish to share with you the key to being truly happy.

If you look at the lives of those you know, how many names can you list for people who are *truly* happy?

Your family? Your boss or co-worker? The friends you know who live in the right part of town and drive a mega-sized SUV?

People living in Cancun in a beach house, who own a Porsche and a ninety-foot yacht?

Famous actors? The rich? Musicians? Politicians?

The President?

For most of us, the list we try to compile will remain a blank sheet of paper with numbers down the left column; or a list of scribbled-out names. This is because, even "the best of us" seek happiness in the wrong avenues.

Happiness is not a matter of living in the right place, nor owning the best clothes, nor driving the latest car, nor having the right friends, nor working the right job.

Happiness is a state of mind.

It is found within us; never without.

It is not a matter of What We Do or What We Own, or even What We Can Create, but always a matter of knowing Who We Are in relationship to ourselves, and God.

As a clear and precise definition, happiness is:

the absence of fear [Satan] and the presence of love [God].

If you can recall the last time you were truly happy, this will ring true.

Perhaps it was that last trip you took, when you "cast your worries upon God", forgetting the stress of home and job while you went to the beach or theme park. Or perhaps it was when your child was born and, at least for a *special moment*, all of life's trials were temporarily forgotten. Or perhaps it occurred while standing in awe of a brilliant sunset, or while watching the fall of silent snow.

Whenever it occurred, whether it lasted for only moments or for days, it was a period in which you were free of everyday worries, and lived with the presence of love and appreciation.

Herein, you have a profound spiritual truth:

By realizing that God will attend to your every "need" – that "need" itself is a concept of "Man" – and that "fear" is the purveyor of "need", you can attain true and lasting happiness.

Whenever we appreciate, we are thanking the Universe for a person, item, or experience. And whatever we thank the Universe for, we have. As spiritual beings, by appreciating, we are experiencing. We are sharing our Life force, and in return are

262

receiving bountiful returns. We are in the absence of fear and in the presence of God's love, and in this, we greet happiness.

As you go about your life after closing these pages, I hope you will strive to appreciate every being – every plant, animal, and human you encounter. In doing so, you can make our world a better place. Water your plants and relish their beauty. Pet your dog or cat and be thankful for their companionship and unconditional love. Tell your loved ones you love them. Say a kind word to everyone you encounter. Smile, and enjoy all that life offers.

Everything needed to bring you happiness is already at hand. God is offering, you need only accept His blessing and love.

Recommended Reading and References:

Albert Einstein: Creator & Rebel
Banesh Hoffman; Copyright 1972
New American Library; Plume
1633 Broadway,
New York, NY 10019

Coincidences: Chance or Fate?
Ken Anderson; Copyright 1991,
A Blandford Book
Cassell plc, Wellington House
125 Strand, London WC2R 0BB

Conversations with God: an uncommon dialogue; book 1
Neale Donald Walsch; Copyright 1995
G.P. Putnam's Sons
200 Madison Avenue
New York, NY 10016

NIV Nave's Topical Bible
John R. Kohlenberger III; Copyright 1992
Zondervan Publishing House
Academic and Professional Books
Grand Rapids, MI 49530

Peter's Quotations: Ideas for Our Time
Dr. Laurence J. Peter; Copyright 1977
Bantam Books, Inc.,
666 Fifth Avenue,
New York, NY 10019

Talking to Heaven: A Medium's Message of Life After Death
James Van Praagh; Copyright 1997
A Signet Book
Penguin Putnam, Inc.,
375 Hudson Street
New York, NY, 10014

The Atom and Beyond: A New Introduction to Modern Physical Science
E. Sheldon Smith; Copyright 1965
Bantam Books, Inc.,
271 Madison Avenue
New York, NY

The Bible
King James Version
The World Publishing Company
2231 West 110th Street
Cleveland 2, Ohio

The Celestine Prophecy: An Adventure
James Redfield; Copyright 1993
Warner Books, Inc.,
1271 Avenue of the Americas
New York, NY 10020

The Celestine Prophecy: An Experiential Guide
James Redfield & Carol Adrienne; Copyright 1995
Warner Books, Inc.,
1271 Avenue of the Americas
New York, NY 10020

The Guideposts Parallel Bible
Copyright 1973,
Zondervan Corporation
Guideposts
Carmel, New York   10512

The Secret Life of Plants
Peter Tompkins and Christopher Bird; Copyright 1973
Harper & Row, Publishers, Inc.,
10 East 53rd Street
New York, NY   10022

You Have Been Here Before
Edith Fiore
Copyright 1978
Ballantine Books,
Div. of Random House, Inc.
New York

Bibliography

[1] Banesh Hoffman: Albert Einstein, Creator and Rebel; 1972; Plume, The Viking Press, NY, NY; pgs 48-53

[2] Albert Einstein, papers published in 1905 and in The Special Theory of Relativity

[3] Tompkins and Bird; The Secret Life of Plants; 1973; Harper and Row Publishers, pgs 18-21

[4] Tompkins and Bird; The Secret Life of Plants; 1973; Harper and Row Publishers, pg 22

[5] James Redfield; The Celestine Prophecy; 1993; Warner Books: 128-131

[6] Quote by Albert Einstein as shown by: www.ludwig.ucl.ac.uk/st/einst.html

[7] http://www.twelvestar.com/Earthlight/Matter%20and%20Energy.html

[8] Terminator 2, Judgement Day; James Cameron; Copyright 1991 Carolco Pictures Inc.; T2 and Terminator are trademarks of Carolco Pictures, Inc., and Carolco Internation, NY

[9] Neale Donald Walsch, Conversations with God, An Uncommon Dialogue, Book 1; 1995; G. P. Putnam's Sons; pg 11

[10] Dale S. Foster; EEG and Subjective Correlates of Alpha-Frequency Binaural-Beat Stimulation Combined with Alpha Biofeedback; http://www.monroe-inst.com/research/alpha-binaural-beat.html

[11] Editor Patricia S. Klein; Miraculous Healings; part of the Hidden Hand of God series, Copyright 2000 by Guideposts, Carmel, New York 10512; Story: The Gift of Hope by Surie Fettman, pgs 14-19

[12] As quoted at: http://www.chesco.com/~artman/einstein.html

[13] Tompkins and Bird; The Secret Life of Plants; 1973; Harper and Row Publishers; pg. 45' appears to be a quote by "Dr. Taut", but the reference to the quote's source is unclear.

[14] Raymond A. Moody, Jr., M.D.; Life After Life, 1975; Bantam Books; pgs. 21-23

[15] James Van Praagh, Talking to Heaven: A Medium's Message of Life After Death; 1997, Signet, pgs. 100-101

[16] Tompkins and Bird; The Secret Life of Plants; 1973; Harper and Row Publishers; (move) pg xi; (living, breathing, communicating) pg. xiv; 14, (awareness) pg. 6,7; (grieve) pg. 13, 14; (remember) pg 9; (track caregivers) pg 10

[17] Evans-Wentz, W. Y. (ed.), The Tibetian Book of the Dead, New York, Oxford University Press, 1957

[18] As quoted at: http://www.chesco.com/~artman/einstein.html

[19] The Merriam-Webster Dictionary; Pocket Books, NY, NY; 1978

[20] One of Einstein's now ubiquitous quotes, often quoted as "God does not play dice" or "God does not play dice with the Cosmos" or "God does not play dice with the Universe". Published in Nature, 1974 and shown at: http://www.automatx.com/einstein.html as quoted in The London Observer,

5 April 1964 http://members.lycos.co.uk/mhertz/index-6.html and numerous other sources.

[21] Neale Donald Walsch, Conversations with God, An Uncommon Dialogue, Book 1; 1995; G. P. Putnam's Sons; page 51-52

[22] As quoted by Alan Vaughan, Incredible Coincidence, The Baffling World of Synchronicity; J. B. Lippincott Co.; pg. 162

[23] Could it be Magic; Barry Manilow, Adrienne Anderson, F. Chopin; Copyright 1977; Arista Records Inc., 6 W. 57th St., NY, NY, 10019

[24] Neale Donald Walsch, Conversations with God, An Uncommon Dialogue, Book 1; 1995; G. P. Putnam's Sons; page 30-32

[25] Albert Einstein, obituary in the New York Times, April 19, 1955

[26] Neale Donald Walsch, Conversations with God, An Uncommon Dialogue, Book 1; 1995; G. P. Putnam's Sons; page 40

[27] Neale Donald Walsch, Conversations with God, An Uncommon Dialogue, Book 1; 1995; G. P. Putnam's Sons; page 42

[28] Dr. Edith Fiore, You Have Been Here Before; 1978; Ballantine Books, NY; pgs 86-147, 191-215